INCREDIBLE STORIES

Zondervan/Youth Specialties Books

INCREDIBLE STORIES

TWENTY ACTIVE BIBLE LESSONS FOR YOUR 8-12 YEAR OLDS

TOM FINLEY

from

Zondervan Publishing House
A Division of HarperCollinsPublishers

Incredible Stories

Copyright ©1991 by Youth Specialties, Inc.

Youth Specialties Books, 1224 Greenfield Drive, El Cajon, California 92021, are published by Zondervan Publishing House, 1415 Lake Drive, S.E., Grand Rapids, Michigan 49506

Library of Congress Cataloging-in-Publication Data

Finley, Tom, 1951-
    Incredible stories: 20 active Bible lessons for your 8-12 year olds / Tom Finley.
       p.   cm. — (Get 'em growing)
      ISBN 0-310-53391-0
      1. Bible—Study. 2. Bible games and puzzles.   I. Title.
II. Series.
BS600.2.F53 1991
268'.432—dc20

90-49315
CIP

Edited by J. Cheri McLaughlin and Kathi George
Design and typography by Mark Rayburn
Illustrated by Tom Finley

Printed in the United States of America

91 92 93 94 95 96 / ML / 6 5 4 3 2 1

THIS ONE'S FOR **TAYLOR**—

WITH LOVE.

About the YOUTHSOURCE™ Publishing Group

YOUTHSOURCE™ books, tapes, videos, and other resources pool the expertise of three of the finest youth ministry resource providers in the world:

❖ **Campus Life Books**—publishers of the award-winning *Campus Life* magazine, who for nearly 50 years have helped high schoolers live Christian lives.

❖ **Youth Specialties**—serving ministers to middle school, junior high, and high school youth for over 20 years through books, magazines, and training events such as the National Youth Workers Convention.

❖ **Zondervan Publishing House**—one of the oldest, largest, and most respected evangelical Christian publishers in the world.

Campus Life
465 Gundersen Dr.
Carol Stream, IL 60188
708/260-6200

Youth Specialties
1224 Greenfield Dr.
El Cajon, CA 92021
619/440-2333

Zondervan
1415 Lake S.E.
Grand Rapids, MI 49506
616/698-6900

TABLE OF INCREDIBLE CONTENTS

PREFACE

The Wrinkled Resource

Teaching God's truth to a roomful of boys and girls—or even a single son or daughter—can be quite a challenge. God made kids with bouncy springs, industrial strength vocal cords, and active minds. While we stolidly proclaim great words of wisdom from the Bible, little bodies wriggle, eyes wander, mouths move, and daydreams thrive.

If our kids were model learners, we think, they would all look, listen, remember, apply—and never speak out of turn. A big *if!* Happily, there are effective methods of captivating the interest of even less-than-perfect learners and teaching them a thing or two. Jesus modeled many of these teaching methods for us: storytelling, object lessons, and discussion questions, for example.

Incredible Stories makes use of two nearly irresistible lures to draw young people into each of 20 terrific Bible stories—that's why *Incredible Stories* gets wrinkled faster than most Bible-teaching resources. First, each story is retold from the point of view of an invented character designed to intrigue the young listener. The story of Achan's sin (Joshua 7), for example, is investigated by a tough-talking private eye. Israel's sin of idolatry (Exodus 32) is reported by a space alien!

Second, after the students hear a story, they are immediately involved in playing a paper game based on the story. These games are the kinds kids like: mazes, rebuses, connect-the-dots, and many more. Why play a game? To attack the truths in each story from an entirely new angle. The act of playing brings players to a clearer understanding of truth and locks the stories into the children's memories.

To round out your teaching time, each story and game comes with a selection of object lessons, thought provokers, and tips that you can use to make the learning experience a rewarding one—destining this book to be the Wrinkled Resource. You'll use it a lot because it's filled with ideas that work!

TOM FINLEY

P.S. Although this book has many features aimed primarily at classroom teaching, moms and dads can use it, too. I'm a dad; I had my kids in mind when I put this together. We've had tons of fun trying it out!

INTRODUCTION

How to Use *Incredible Stories*

Using this book is almost like cooking from a recipe. Read a story, play a game, throw in some special spices, and . . . presto! You can serve up nutritious Bible wisdom, topped with comprehension of the subject and retention of the important points.

Incredible Stories has 20 Bible stories, each with a fun paper game to photocopy and distribute. By combining a story, a game, and some or all of the extra tips and ideas suggested, you can put together a wonderful learning experience—a spiritual meal—ranging from 20 minutes to as much as an hour. The actual time span is up to you.

Cooking with *Incredible Stories*

First Ingredient—the Story

The Bible will come alive to your young listeners as you read these fun stories. Each takes five to ten minutes to read. At the beginning of every story, you'll find the related Bible passage, the spiritual theme of the lesson, and a suggested Story Starter to grab your students' attention. Be sure to prepare beforehand by reading the original story in your Bible.

When it comes to telling stories, we all have our own styles. Perhaps you like to nearly memorize the tale and leave the book on the shelf. Or maybe you prefer to read it word for word. Both ways work well; do what is most comfortable for you. Using the following tips, however, can add zest to anybody's style of storytelling.

❖ *Embellish the stories.* Throw in a few sound effects. Jump off the furniture. Chew up the scenery. If you have fun, so will your listeners.

❖ *Use eye contact, dramatic pauses, voice characterization, and pacing* (fast in the dramatic moments, slower in the profound) to capture and keep your students' interest.

❖ *Ask questions of the learners as you read* to make sure they understand what's going on in the stories. One story, for example, casts you (the narrator) as a prosecuting attorney. Ask your listeners if they know what that is. In another story, the main character works in a drainpipe. You might ask kids who have crawled down a drainpipe to tell what they found there.

❖ *Invite your students to ask questions of you while you read.*

❖ *Retell some stories in your own words.* Tailor our tales to suit your personality and the needs of your learners.

❖ *Present a story as a skit* with the help of other adults or older students. Some of the stories can be easily adapted to script format, and your learners remember better what they both see and hear.

Second Ingredient—the Game

Each game consists of two parts. Complete on one page is the players' game sheet. Photocopy enough game sheets to hand out one to each player or group of players. On a separate page are instructions to the teacher, including a list of materials required and approximate playing time. Provide any materials required (pencils, scissors, old magazines). Tables, magazines, or even the floor can be used as a playing surface.

When ready to play, read the instructions aloud and be sure everyone understands them. The time required to play the games varies, but ranges from about five to 15 minutes. The games are not competitive in nature; however, you may offer a small prize to anyone who completes a particular game. Kids love that sort of motivation! When everyone has attempted to complete the game, you may wish to post a copy of the game's solution; you'll find the solutions to the more difficult games at the end of this book.

Why play games? Kids love to play games and solve puzzles. Here are the benefits of allowing your children to do so.

❖ Each game reviews and reinforces the important spiritual points of the related Bible story.

❖ The action required by the game—searching for the solution, putting the brain in gear, writing out key words from the story—makes it easier for the players to retain what they have learned from the story.

❖ By discussing or viewing the completed game, you can readily measure the effectiveness of your teaching. If the students have succeeded with the game, they have learned the lesson.

❖ Working together helps build friendships. Although all of the games can be played by one player alone, we recommend that you have children play in groups (two or three together). If you are a parent with one child, play the game with your child.

Final Ingredient—the Special Spices

Every story/game combination comes with a set of red-hot tips and suggestions to use as you see fit. As space allows, we'll give you object lessons, craft ideas, extra-credit games, related Scripture passages, and creative concluding activities. We've even included discussion questions. Don't worry if your kids aren't great contributors. Questions are only one of several ways to drive home biblical truths. Be sure to encourage children who do join in the discussions, even if their remarks are a bit off the track.

Bible Stories, Games, and Ideas:

When you put them all together . . . they spell
A great spiritual meal to nourish young believers.

1. God Is Creator of the Universe

> **Bible Passage:** Genesis 1:1-27.
> **Lesson Theme:** God made everything—including us—with a purpose in mind.

STORY

Story Starter: You might like to start with the Object Lesson. When you are ready to read the story, tell your listeners about the greatest thing you ever made (dress, recipe, woodwork project). Ask kids to relate the great things they have made. Say something like, *You're all so creative! I think people are creative because God, who made us, is the greatest creator of all. Let's imagine we are listening in on a conversation that takes place in a very unusual little store called the Creation Store.*

"Ding-a-ling," cheerfully rang the little bell over the shop door as a customer entered. The jolly-looking proprietor came around the counter. "Good morning, sir. Welcome to the Creation Store. How may I help you?"

"Well, I'm feeling very creative today," replied the customer. "I think I'd like to create something. Yes, I would. I'd like to create something."

"You've come to the right place, sir," said the shop owner. "This is the Creation Store, devoted to one purpose—helping creative people turn ideas into existence. Just what did you have in mind? If you'll tell me, we can fix you right up with everything you need. We have some lovely subatomic particles on sale, sir. Marked down to $2.99 each. That's just 200 trillion billion dollars a thimbleful."

The customer ignored the sales pitch. "I think I'd like to create light," he said. "Yes, light sounds good. I'll shine it on things so people can see. A good idea, don't you think? No more stumbling about in the darkness."

The proprietor displayed a weak smile. "I'm so very sorry, sir. Light has already been created. You're just a smidgeon too late. The Lord God said, `Let there be light,' and there was light."

"Light has been created?" responded the disappointed customer. "Pity. Well, perhaps I'll create something else. I have it! I'll make the sky. Yes, the sky is very good. It will hold the clouds up and people can breathe it."

"Sorry. It's been done. God made that, too."

"Been done? Okay, then how about this? I'll create land. People need something to walk on, you know."

"God beat you to it."

"The seas?"

"That, too."

"Vegetation? Trees and things?"

"Yes. God again."

"The sun, moon, and stars?"

"He did those ages ago, sir."

"Fish?"

"Fish."

"What about birds? Marvelous idea, birds. Couldn't I just . . . ?"

"He's done birds already, I'm afraid."

"Well, animals then. I'll do animals. Furry things. Four legs."

"Already taken care of, sir. Furry ones, smooth ones, four-legged ones, animals with no legs. The list goes on and on, sir."

"Now, wait just a minute. It sounds like everything has been created already. God has done it all!"

"I'm afraid you're right, sir. Everything has been created. Almighty God did it long ago. Why, he even created you and me, sir. He merely spoke the word and everything came into existence."

"Well, that's a fine how-do-you-do. If he's created everything there is, how can a store like yours stay in business?"

"That is a problem, sir. In fact, right now I'm creating a going-out-of-business sale."

After the Story: Explain to your students that the things mentioned in the story are many of the things mentioned in the biblical account of creation: light, atmosphere, land, vegetation. If time allows, read Genesis 1:1 through 2:2.

You may wish to amaze your learners with a few facts about God's creation. There are 100 billion stars in our Milky Way galaxy. At one star per second, it would take more than 3,000 years to count them all. There are possibly as many galaxies of stars as there are stars in our galaxy. A drop of water contains 100 billion billion atoms. A pulse of light could travel around the earth about eight times in one second. It would take 2.5 billion billion billion candles to be as bright as the sun. Working for years to determine the distance to galaxies in the universe, scientists have mapped just one one-hundred-thousandth (.00001) of the volume of space.

GAME INSTRUCTIONS

Materials Needed: One photocopy of the game per player, pencils.

Approximate Playing Time: 8-10 minutes.

Special Instructions: Hand out copies of the game. Let students work in pairs. Read the instructions aloud, and be sure everyone understands the example of EARVENS and HEATH. Use poster paper or chalkboard to show how the words are split and recombined. This game isn't as hard as it might sound, but you can make it even easier by providing Bibles or a list of the words to look for.

After the Game: Review the solution (heavens, earth, light, sky, land, seas, plants, trees, sun, moon, stars, fish, birds, animals, Adam, Eve). Ask the game's extra-credit question: "Do you know what *genesis* means?" The answer is *beginnings*.

Materials Needed:

Object lesson: various household items, including some unusual ones.

Learning project: clothes hangers, magazine pictures, paste, crayons, scissors, drawing paper, string.

Conclusion activity: construction paper, crayons, scissors, felt pens.

Discussion Starters: Why do you think Genesis is called "the book of beginnings"? Why do you suppose God made everything? Why did he create people? Do you think he might have a special purpose for each of us? What are some things he might want us to do?

Object Lesson: Bring several items to class, such as tools, kitchen utensils, and tubes of makeup. Ask kids to describe the purpose of each item. (It's great fun if you can find mysterious things like antique radio tubes.) Explain that God has a purpose for everything he created, including each student. Describe some of the good things God wants us to be, do, and experience.

Learning Project: Students can make a poster or mobile (with clothes hangers) of things God created. Let them use paste and magazine pictures or their own drawings.

Extra-Credit Game: Play "Twenty Questions," challenging your students to guess an object you have in mind, something God created.

Conclusion Activity: Request pairs of students to create a thank-you card to God for his creation.

GOD MADE IT, WE BROKE IT!

*In the beginning God created the heavens and the earth
(Genesis 1:1).*

God made everything. The first two chapters of the Bible list a bunch of things he put together. For example, the first verse of the Bible, quoted above, tells us that God made the heavens and the earth.

Many of the things mentioned in Genesis are listed below. Just one problem. We dropped the list and broke each word into two parts. When we tried to put the words back together, we messed everything up. Please help us! Split each nonsense word into two parts, and then stick them back together to make the correct words. Here's an example: HEATH and EARVENS can be split apart and put together as HEAVENS and EARTH. It's up to you to figure out where to divide each nonsense word.

HEATH
EARVENS
SIGHT
LKY
SAND
LEAS

PLEES
TRANTS
SMALS
MOE
STON
FIRDS
ANISH
BIARS
ADUN
EVAM

WRITE THE CORRECT WORDS IN THIS BOX.

EXTRA-CREDIT QUESTION: Do you know what the word *genesis* means?

2. A Serpent in the Garden

Bible Passage: Genesis 3:1-19.
Lesson Theme: How sin entered the universe; how a believer's sin can be forgiven.

STORY

Story Starter: Show your students an apple or other fruit. Tell them something like, *See this apple? It's good to eat; delicious. I'm tempted to eat it. A simple piece of fruit like this and the temptation to eat it led to the biggest problem the universe has ever known! Can you guess what that problem is? The story I'm about to read will help you with the answer.*

Picture yourselves as the jury in an imaginary courtroom. On trial is someone accused of purposely lying with the intent to lead millions of people to their deaths. The accused will act as his own attorney. His name is Satan. It is your job to listen to the evidence and decide whether Satan is guilty or innocent.

The prosecuting attorney is ready to bring criminal charges against Satan. Listen as the trial begins. He is calling two witnesses: their names are Adam and Eve. He looks at the lady seated in the witness box.

"Eve, tell the court in your own words exactly what happened on that fateful day when the serpent spoke to you."

"Objection! She's lying!" Satan shouted, leaping up from his chair near the front of the courtroom.

"Objection overruled, Satan. She hasn't even said anything yet. Now, Eve, please answer the question."

"Well, I was taking a walk in the garden—that's the garden of Eden, where God had originally placed Adam and me—when all of a sudden a serpent hissed at me. I knew he wanted to speak to me, so I stopped."

"Didn't it seem strange to you that an animal might speak?"

"Not really. You see, everything that God had made for us was so new and full of surprises that a talking animal seemed quite natural. I thought it was just one more of God's wonderful gifts."

"What did the serpent say?"

"He asked if it was true that God told me not to eat fruit from any tree in the garden."

"And is that what God had said?"

"No. He said we could eat of all the trees except one, the tree of the knowledge of good and evil. God said Adam and I would die if we ate from that one."

"And you told this to the serpent?"

"Yes. But I changed what God said, too. I added that God had told us to not even touch the tree. By that time, I was so mixed up I couldn't remember what God had said."

"So God had said you would die if you ate from the tree of the knowledge of good and evil. What did the serpent say about this?"

"He claimed that God had lied. He said that I would not die. He also said God knew that if I ate from the tree I would become like God, knowing all about good and evil."

"And what happened next?"

"Like a fool, I believed the serpent's lies. I thought I could become wise like God. I told Adam and we ate from the tree. Oh, I'm so ashamed." Eve breaks down in tears. The prosecutor helps her from the witness stand.

"I call as my next witness, Adam. Adam, tell us what happened."

"It's just like Eve said. We ate the fruit and suddenly realized that we had disobeyed God. We ran for cover. God found us hiding among the trees. He was very displeased. He punished the serpent for lying to us."

"Can you point out the serpent in this room?"

Adam turns to face the accused. "He's the one: Satan!"

In a rush, Satan stands. "Yes. I was the serpent. I lied to Eve and caused her and Adam to sin against God. I hate God and I hate you all!"

After the judge restores order, the prosecutor says, "Ladies and gentlemen of the jury, let me sum up the evidence for you. We've heard testimony to the following. One, Satan disguised himself as a serpent in order to gain Eve's confidence. Two, he cast doubts into her mind by misquoting what the Lord had said about which trees could be eaten from. Three, he told Eve that God was a liar, claiming that she would not die if she ate the forbidden fruit. Four, Satan accused God of trying to prevent Adam and Eve from becoming like him. Five, Satan made a false promise by suggesting that Adam and Eve ever could become like God.

"And what were the results of all this? The world has been plunged into sin ever since that day. Ladies and gentlemen of the jury, you must make your decision. Is Satan guilty or innocent?"

After the Story: Ask your learners to decide by vote if Satan is guilty as accused. You may point out the immediate results of Adam and Eve's rebellion: they became aware of their nakedness and were ashamed (lost their innocence); they grew afraid of God, whom they had loved; they hid from God; God cursed the serpent; God told Eve that childbirth would be painful and marriage would be a struggle; he told Adam that weeds and hard work would replace the easy life he had known; animals were killed to make clothing; Adam and Eve (and humanity) were banished from Eden and cut off from the tree of life.

The spiritual results were the worst of all. Sin entered creation, and humanity has suffered physical and spiritual death ever since.

GAME INSTRUCTIONS

Materials Needed: One photocopy of the game per player, coins for game markers.

Approximate Playing Time: 5 minutes. This game can be played several times.

Special Instructions: Hand out copies of the game. For markers, each of the two or three players at one game board needs a different type of coin. The object is for players to avoid moving their coins into the Bite the Apple space. (We've used an apple to symbolize the forbidden fruit. Explain that no one knows what kind of fruit it actually was.)

Tell players the following instructions: ***This game will help you remember the story of Adam and Eve. Put your coins on Start. Players move their coins ahead only one space each turn. Notice that there are large spaces that contain statements such as, "The serpent talks to you," and arrows pointing to Heads or Tails. When you land on one of these large spaces, flip your coin to see which arrow to follow. The arrows will lead you either toward or away from the Bite the Apple space. If you land there, you are out of the game. The last person left is the winner.***

After the Game: Discuss the meaning and significance of the statements in the large spaces on the game board, relating the statements to how Satan behaves today.

TEACHING IDEAS

Materials Needed:

Learning project: paper large enough to cover Bible, colored pens or pencils, card stock for Bible verse booklets.

Discussion Starters: Satan is guilty of bringing sin to humanity. But what about Adam and Eve—are they guilty of anything? If so, what? (The Bible makes it clear that all people are guilty of sin and will be called to judgment. See Romans 3:23 and Hebrews 9:27.) If we are all guilty of sin, is there a way we can be completely pardoned and go to heaven? (See Hebrews 9:28 for the answer.)

Define your terms: As you involve your students in the following discussion, be sure they understand the concepts of sin and salvation.

Learning Project: If your students have Bibles, let them make covers out of paper. Have them label the covers with titles such as, "God's Word—Important Facts Inside!" or "Read Once a Day to Keep the Devil Away."

If they don't have their own Bibles, have them make "mini-Bibles" by copying some important verses (John 3:16, for instance) onto folded card stock.

Extra-Credit Game: Emphasize that Eve sinned partly because she did not have a clear idea of what God had told her; she misquoted him and believed the devil when he mis-

quoted God. The following test will demonstrate to your students that they may not know the Bible—God's Word—as well as they could. Read the list of familiar quotes below, and ask your class to vote on which ones are actually from the Bible.

1. "Cleanliness is next to godliness."
2. "Just say no."
3. "Man does not live on bread alone." *Matthew 4:4*
4. "Everything is possible for him who believes." *Mark 9:23*
5. "A mighty fortress is our God."
6. "Idle hands are the devil's tool."
7. "Blessed are the merciful, for they will be shown mercy." *Matthew 5:7*
8. "My breath is offensive to my wife." *Job 19:17*

Conclusion Activity: If you did the learning project, have students display and explain their efforts. Read 1 John 1:9. Tell your learners that even though sin is the worst problem in the universe, Christ's death on the cross and God's forgiveness have solved the problem for believers.

Finish this lesson on a happy note by reading Revelation 22:1-5. Explain that the scene is heaven after Jesus has come again. The tree of life that was lost to us when Adam and Eve sinned is given back to those of us who are saved by faith in Christ.

DON'T BITE THAT APPLE!

"Did God really say, 'You must not eat from any tree in the garden'?"
(Genesis 3:1).

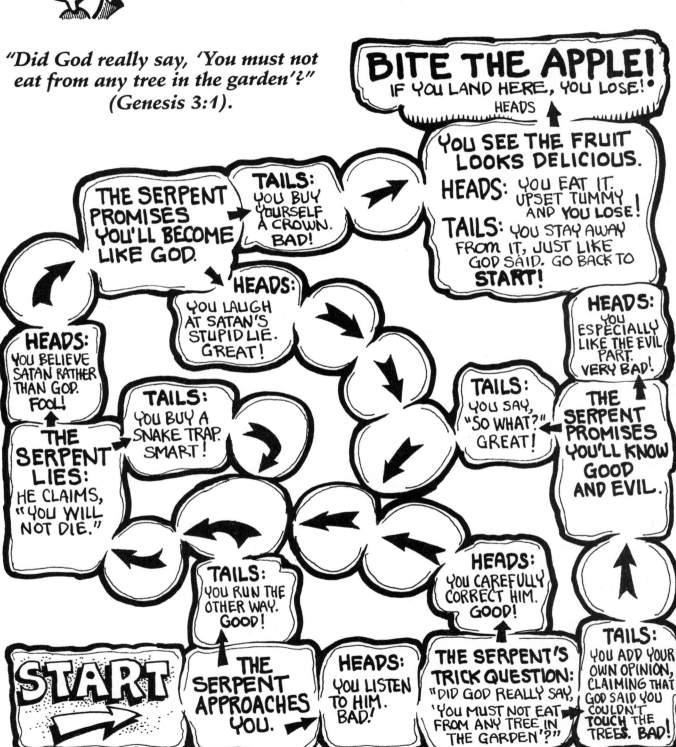

3. Noah's Ark

Bible Passage: Genesis 6:11-8:22.
Lesson Theme: The ark provided salvation from judgment; faith in Christ saves us now.

STORY

Story Starter: The Extra-Credit Game makes a nice opening. The game concerns animals, which are closely connected with Noah and the ark. Or, talk about the worst rainstorm you were ever in or a time you nearly drowned.

Since the story of Noah's ark is well known by most children, the following story doesn't give all the details. Rather it provides you with an opportunity to compare with your children the type of salvation the ark provided and the salvation Jesus provides. You may want to summarize the biblical details after you read the story.

When you're ready to begin, ask your students if they have ever watched one of those TV shows dedicated to Hollywood entertainment. Tell them you want to read a story that supposedly takes place on one of those shows.

"Good evening, and thank you for watching *Entertaining News,* the show that lets you in on all the gossip about Hollywood stars and celebrities. I'm Gloria Eyelash, in Hollywood.

"All this week we've been reporting on the filming of Hollywood's latest blockbuster movie, *Noah's Ark.* Let's go to this live report from Hollywood correspondent Dan Dentalfloss. Dan?"

"Thank you, Gloria. I don't know if you can hear me, Gloria. I'm shouting as loud as I can. There seems to be a problem with the thousands of animals that are here for the filming of *Noah's Ark.* Of course, you know that God told Noah to bring his family and many animals on board the ark. A couple of minutes ago, two mice broke out of their cage. The cats got loose and started chasing the mice. The dogs started chasing the cats. The zebras are chasing the dogs. I think they're coming this way, Gloria. I think I need to . . . oh, oh. The lions are loose! The lions are chasing the zebras that are chasing the dogs that are chasing the cats that are chasing the mice. The elephants have jumped out of their corral. The elephants are chasing the lions. The elephants are knocking over the rest of the cages. Thousands of animals are free. And they're all chasing me! Help!"

"Dan? Dan? This is Gloria Eyelash, Dan. Can you hear me?"

"Whew! Yes, Gloria. I'm okay now, I think. Just a little breathless. The camera crew and I jumped into the elephant corral, which is now empty. Here with me now is Aaron Spielberg, the producer and director of this Hollywood extravaganza. Aaron, what scene are you about to film now?"

"This is the most important part of the movie—the flood scene. This is where God sends the rain and the floods on the earth. The ark, with Noah, Noah's family, and all the animals on board, rises up on the surface of the waters. If everything goes according to plan, our ark, a full-scale replica of the original, will ride the giant flood that we are about to recreate. As you can see, we've spared no expense."

"It's truly amazing, Aaron. You've built the ark right in front of these giant floodgates. When you open the gates, thousands of tons of water will sweep through this beautiful rural valley—destroying everything for miles around."

"That is correct. I've got ten cameras ready to capture it on film. But now, we'd all better get on board the ark. It's the only safe place to be, Mr. Dentalfloss."

"Just like the original ark, eh? God told Noah to build the ark and take his family and the animals aboard so that they could survive the end of the world back then. Let's climb aboard.

"Well, Gloria, we're on the ark now. Aaron Spielberg has just radioed the order to open the floodgates. Here comes the water. The flood is hitting the ark. It's moving . . . no, wait! The ark is breaking open! It almost looks like it's melting in the water. This is horrible! Mr. Spielberg, Mr. Spielberg! Glub, blub! Why is the ark falling apart?"

"It's those idiots in the prop department. They made the ark out of papier-mâché! Blub. . . ."

"This is Gloria Eyelash. Tune in next week, when *Entertaining News* will cover *The End of the World*, the new film from producer Francis Lucas. So long, everybody."

GAME INSTRUCTIONS

Materials Needed: Several photocopies of the game for each player, pencils.

Approximate Playing Time: 2-3 minutes per round. Play several rounds as time permits.

Special Instructions: Be sure to play this game yourself before asking the class to play it. Players will want to play this game more than once, so provide each player with several copies of the game (or a good eraser). Let students play in teams of two or three, each team member working on a separate copy of the game. The team selects the highest score they can come up with.

When you're ready to begin say, *Listen carefully while I tell you how to play. Look at your game sheets. You are to help Noah load his ark by drawing a pencil line along the paths from the edge of the approaching floodwaters to the ark at the top. Each time your pencil line crosses a person (one of Noah's family members) or an animal, that person or animal gets to board the ark. Your job is to load as many people and animals on the ark as possible.*

There are two important rules that make this game a bit tough. First, the line you draw must never cross itself (except by bridge). Second, you cannot use the same section of path more than once. The sample game shows what I mean. When you finally enter the ark, add up your score by giving yourself one point for each person or animal your line crossed. It is not possible to get them all, but you can try!

After the Game: Display the suggested solution from the solution sheet at the back of the book. That solution is not necessarily the highest score possible.

TEACHING IDEAS

Materials Needed:

Conclusion activity: one sheet poster board, scissors for all, paste, magazines with animal pictures.

Discussion Starters: Find a microphone or something that looks like a microphone. Pretend you are a reporter conducting interviews with the animals as they disembark the ark after the flood. Your students pretend they are the animals (one young man we interviewed said he was a fly). Start with simple, silly questions like, "Did you get seasick?" Move into thought-provoking questions such as, "People who got on the ark were saved from the flood—what does becoming a Christian save us from?" and "Why do people need to be spiritually saved?" (These harder questions can be asked of the whole group.)

Extra-Credit Game: A silly action game— "Moose, Moose"—will get your kids excited about this session. Seat everyone in a circle. The first player says, "Moose, moose," and at

the same time uses his or her hands to make antlers, signifying a moose. The player then points to someone else who must say, "Moose, moose," make the antlers, and then name another animal (like "Cat, cat"), making an appropriate sign (such as using fingers for whiskers). That player then points to another player. Play goes on with each player saying the names of all the animals and making the signs, then adding a new animal. Players who mess up are out of the game. Start a new round each time someone goes out. Preplan some animal signals to suggest to your students.

Conclusion Activity: Provide one sheet of poster board, scissors for everyone, paste, and magazines with animal pictures. (To save time, you can cut out the pictures before class.) Each child pastes at least one animal to the poster board. Title the board with a message like, "The Ark Saved Noah and the Animals; Jesus Saves Us!"

HARK, AN ARK!

"You will enter the ark—you and your sons and your wife and your sons' wives with you. You are to bring into the ark two of all living creatures, male and female, to keep them alive with you" (Genesis 6:18, 19).

The rules:

1. Draw your line through as many people and animals as you can.
2. Your line cannot cross itself except by bridge.
3. You cannot use the same section of path more than once.

Sample game:

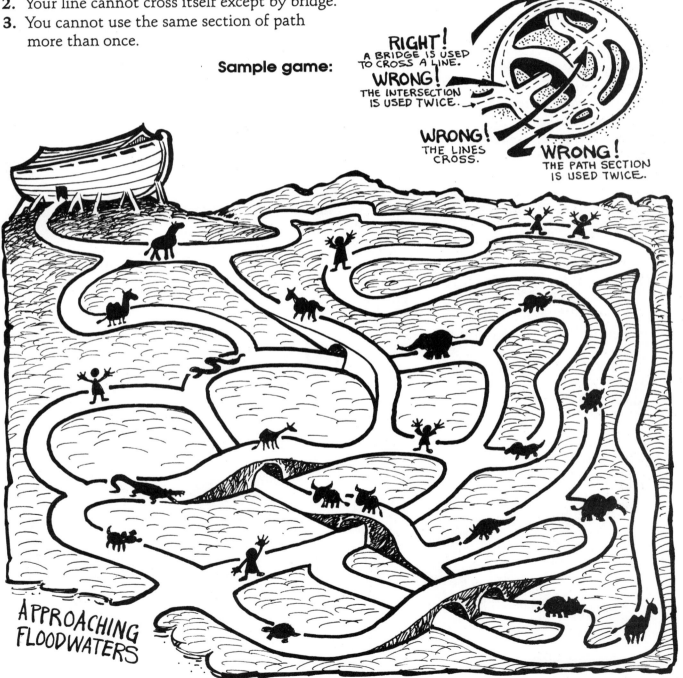

RIGHT!
A BRIDGE IS USED TO CROSS A LINE.

WRONG!
THE INTERSECTION IS USED TWICE.

WRONG!
THE LINES CROSS.

WRONG!
THE PATH SECTION IS USED TWICE.

APPROACHING FLOODWATERS

4. The Plagues of Egypt

Bible Passage: Exodus 7:14-11:10.
Lesson Theme: Pharaoh's hard heart and God's sovereignty.

STORY

Story Starter: Ask your listeners if they enjoy getting letters in the mail. Find out if they like to write letters. Who do they write to? What do they write about? Say something like, *I enjoy sending and receiving mail, too. In a minute I'm going to read you some letters written by an imaginary son to his mother, a long time ago in the days of Moses.*

Do you remember Moses? God told him to lead the children of Israel out of Egypt, where they were slaves, to the freedom of the Promised Land. But there was one big problem— Pharaoh, the king of Egypt, did not want to lose his slaves. He was not about to let Moses or the children of Israel go. But God had an idea. He would cause Pharaoh and Egypt so much trouble that the king would beg Moses and the people to leave.

Let's pretend that we are back in the days of Moses, reading some letters that have been mailed by an Egyptian young man to his mother. In these letters, he describes what the Bible tells us God did and how Pharaoh responded.

❖ ❖ ❖

Dear Mummy:
 I hope you're enjoying your vacation. Things have been going well here, except for one strange thing. Today in the newspaper it said that Moses told Pharaoh to let the Israelites go. If the king refused, Moses said the God of Israel was going to turn all the water in Egypt into blood!
 This is the same newspaper that prints stories about flying saucers and babies that look like camels. So I figured it was silly, right? Well, guess what? The waters turned to blood! That's right! The Nile is red. All the fish are dead. And the smell! Yech! Even my orange soda turned red. I'll let you know what happens.
 Love,
 Your Son Akbed

Dear Mom:
 It's been a week since I last wrote. In case you're wondering, Pharaoh did not let Moses and the people go. We were able to find some drinking water, so everything seems fine. Wait a minute, someone's at the door. Okay, I'm back. It was just a couple of frogs hopping against the door. That reminds me, someone told me Moses said that God would send a plague of frogs if Pharaoh didn't let the people go. Frogs, can you believe it? Ha!
 Wait, now someone's at the window. Eek! Frogs! Thousands of them leaping in the window. I've got to write fast, Ma. I can hardly hear myself think for all the croaking. I wish these stupid toads would shut up. Hey, they're jumping on my bed. Oh no, now they're in the refrigerator. They're playing my stereo!
 I'll write later.
 Akbed

Dear Mom,

I hop . . . I mean I hope you're having a better time than we are. The frogs were bad enough, but now guess what? Gnats. What harm can a few gnats do, you say? Ma, they're everywhere. They're on all the animals. They're on all the people. Ma, I have them in my teeth! Gaaaa!

Akbed

Mom:

Can you believe it? Blood, frogs, and gnats, and still Pharaoh won't let Moses and his people go. Let them go, I say. But you haven't heard the worst yet. After the gnats came flies. Swarms of biting flies. I have the bandages to prove it. Then all the livestock died. Every horse, donkey, and camel in Egypt dropped dead. All of them except the ones that belonged to the children of Israel. Not one of theirs died. And if that wasn't enough, boils! Festering, yucky boils on everybody's skin. It's not a pretty sight.

Sincerely,
Akbed

Mom:

It hailed a couple days ago. Pharaoh still hasn't let Moses go, even though the hail killed every person and every animal outdoors. Luckily, I was in here writing to you. I would have saved some hail in the refrigerator like I used to do when I was a kid, but the hailstones were too big. Sorry about your chariot. It was parked outdoors.

Akbed

Mom:

Well, I suppose I could complain about the plague of locusts. They came in swarms and devoured every tree and crop that hadn't been wiped out by the hail. I heard that Pharaoh's advisors begged him to let Moses go. But he didn't.

And I suppose I could cry about the three days of total darkness that covered Egypt. The Israelites had light, of course. Their God is one tough guy.

But you ain't heard nothin' yet. Today, Moses said that God would kill the firstborn son of every Egyptian family if Pharaoh doesn't let the children of Israel leave for their Promised Land. Moses said that the firstborn would all die tonight at midnight. It's almost that time now. I can hear the clock ticking. Time's almost up. I can hear the chime. It's striking twel . . . Arrrrgghh!

❖ ❖ ❖

GAME INSTRUCTIONS

Materials Needed: One photocopy of the game per player, pencils.

Approximate Playing Time: 10-15 minutes. It's not necessary to allow all players to finish the game.

Special Instructions: Hand out the game. The children can use the plague cartoons at the bottom of the game sheet to guide them as they unscramble the words. Or you can fold the sheet to hide the cartoons until players have finished unscrambling.

After the Game: Review the answers to the scrambled words (*blood, frogs, gnats, flies, livestock, boils, hail, locusts, darkness, firstborn*). Congratulate all players for their efforts.

TEACHING IDEAS

Materials Needed:

Learning project: pencils with erasers, enough small notepads so that every group of two students has one.

Conclusion activity: pencils, lined stationery.

Discussion Starters: Why did Moses and the children of Israel want to leave Egypt? Why didn't Pharaoh want them to go? What did God do to change Pharaoh's mind? In this story, do you think God seemed weak, powerful, or very powerful? If you were an Egyptian and saw God do all these powerful things, would you want to make friends with God? How can we become God's friend today?

Object Lesson: Explain that God used Pharaoh's hard heart to demonstrate God's incredible power. Read Proverbs 21:1, "The king's heart is in the hand of the Lord; he directs it like a watercourse wherever he pleases." Show or describe a water faucet or a wall switch. Say, **God is so powerful, he can change the heart of even the most powerful rulers on earth just as easily as we turn a faucet or flip a switch. For God, it's easy. He's in charge; he's in control.** Turn the faucet or flip the switch several times.

Learning Project: A favorite kids' game is to make an "animated cartoon" by drawing a simple figure on each of several dozen pages of a small notepad. When the pages are flipped, the figure moves. Allow students to work in pairs to animate a cartoon that shows power. Some students might draw a stick of dynamite exploding. Others might animate the faucet from the object lesson. Still others could show one of the plagues, such as a swarm of gnats (dots) moving across the page. Give students five or ten minutes to complete the project, then discuss how each cartoon relates to God's strength and power.

Conclusion Activity: Ask students to think of one area in their lives where they would like to see God's power demonstrated (a problem at home, a prayer request, a material need). Each student then jots a private note to God, asking him to demonstrate his great power in this area. If you enjoy a close relationship with your young learners, tell them you would be happy to talk with them privately about these areas.

BLAST THAT HARD HEART!

PHARAOH AND HIS HARD HEART.

The Lord had said to Moses, "Pharaoh will refuse to listen to you—so that my wonders may be multiplied in Egypt" (Exodus 11:9).

God had to deal harshly with Pharaoh. He sent ten terrible plagues to convince the hard-hearted ruler to let Moses and the children of Israel leave Egypt. Even so, it took all ten before Pharaoh gave in.

For extra fun, this game has two parts. First, unscramble the words in the list to find the ten plagues. Next, place the point of your pencil on one of the plague cartoons at the bottom of the page. With your eyes closed, try to draw a line from the plague to Pharaoh up above. Open your eyes to see how you did. If your line ends on Pharaoh, give yourself ten points. If you missed, subtract two points and try again. After you've blasted Pharaoh's hard heart with all ten plagues, add up your score.

UNSCRAMBLE THESE PLAGUES:

SLOIB

DOLOB

NASESRKD

ANGST

VILEKCTOS

ALIH

SORGF   NORBSTRIF   USCLOST   LESIF

5. The Passover

Bible Passage: Exodus 12:1-12, 21-30.
Lesson Theme: Blood has been shed on
our behalf.

STORY

Story Starter: Try the Extra-Credit Game to let students discover the story's subject. When ready to begin the story, tell your learners, *We're going to hear a story about the first Passover. You might not know what Passover is now, but you will when the story is over. Our tale takes place in a cave carved into a mountain. The cave served as a tomb. Inside the tomb are two people. Two living people, that is.*

"Uncle Joshua, tell me again how you became a grave cleaner."

Uncle Joshua smiled and paused to lean on his broom. He enjoyed telling this story to his young niece Miriam, for maintaining graves was a job that his family had proudly done for generations. Having no children of his own, he hoped that Miriam would carry on when he was gone. She was a good apprentice and displayed a great deal of potential.

"It started centuries ago," he began, "back in my great, great, oh-so-very great grandfather's day." Miriam adjusted the torch in order to see her Uncle Joshua's old, rugged face in the darkness of the tomb they were cleaning.

"It was back in the days of the first Passover," continued Uncle Joshua. "The Passover is one of the most important dates in Jewish history, Miriam. God did something strange and terrifying to the Egyptians in order to finally force Pharaoh to let Moses and the children of Israel leave Egypt."

"Tell me about it, Uncle Joshua," pleaded Miriam.

"I can do better than that, girl," smiled Uncle Joshua. "I can quote it from the Scriptures by memory."

Moses summoned all the elders of Israel and said to them, "Go at once and select the animals for your families and slaughter the Passover lamb. Take a bunch of hyssop, dip it into the blood in the basin and put some of the blood on the top and both sides of the doorframe. Not one of you shall go out the door of his house until morning. When the Lord goes through the land to strike down the Egyptians, he will see the blood on the top and sides of the doorframe and will pass over that doorway, and he will not permit the destroyer to enter your houses and strike you down.

"Obey these instructions as a lasting ordinance for you and your descendants. When you enter the land that the Lord will give you as he promised, observe this ceremony. And when your children ask you, 'What does this ceremony mean to you?' then tell them, 'It is the Passover sacrifice to the Lord, who passed over the houses of the Israelites in Egypt and spared our homes when he struck down the

Egyptians.'" Then the people bowed down and worshiped. The Israelites did just what the Lord commanded Moses and Aaron.

At midnight the Lord struck down all the firstborn in Egypt, from the firstborn of Pharaoh, who sat on the throne, to the firstborn of the prisoner, who was in the dungeon, and the firstborn of all the livestock as well. Pharaoh and all his officials and all the Egyptians got up during the night, and there was loud wailing in Egypt, for there was not a house without someone dead (Exodus 12:21-30).

"And that," said Uncle Joshua, "was how Passover came to be. God told Moses that he was about to kill the firstborn Egyptians. The Israelites would be spared by sacrificing lambs and putting the blood on their doorposts. The Lord passed over all the Israelite homes, because the blood of the lambs was a sign to God."

Miriam looked thoughtful. "You're right about what you said, Uncle. God had to do a strange and terrifying thing to the Egyptians. And that was when your great, great, oh-so-very-great grandfather began working with graves. He must have had a lot of work, with all those dead Egyptians lying about."

Uncle Joshua sighed. "I'm afraid not, lass. He was a child of Israel, don't forget. Moses and the Israelites fled Egypt immediately. He had to leave with them. No, I'm afraid that great, great, oh-so-very great grandfather got a very slow start. There were no Jewish graves at that Passover."

"And now, many years later, it's Passover again," commented Miriam. All week long, Israel had been celebrating the Passover festival in memory of what God did.

"Yes," agreed the old man. "And I'm wondering if perhaps God passed over this tomb today."

"What do you mean?"

"This tomb is empty. There's supposed to be a body in here. But there is no body."

Miriam gasped. "Who's supposed to be buried here?"

"A man named Jesus."

After the Story: Just before playing the game, discuss with your students the fact that Jesus died for us during a Passover week. Just as the lamb's blood caused God to pass over the Israelites, Christ's blood, shed for us on the cross, saves believers today.

GAME INSTRUCTIONS

Materials Needed: One photocopy of the game for each team of two or three players, pencils.

Approximate Playing Time: 5 minutes.

Special Instructions: Gather players into groups of two or three, distributing one game sheet to each group. Have everyone jot answers on their game sheets. If you prefer, you can read the poetry aloud to the class and let students shout out suggested rhymes.

After the Game: Read completed poems and discuss the important points. Possible rhyming words to complete the poem are, in order: *know, mine, dead, died, heaven.*

Materials Needed:

Learning project: poster paper with verse written on it, index cards with one word each, tape.

Extra-credit game: poster paper or chalkboard.

Conclusion activity: one Band-Aid per learner.

Discussion Starters: What was the sign that saved Moses and the Israelites from death? Without the blood, what would have happened to them? In what way is the blood on the doorposts connected to Jesus? Without the death of Jesus, what would have happened to us? Why do you suppose it's important that Jesus came alive after his death?

Learning Project: Here is a simple challenge that kids seem to really enjoy. Before class, write Acts 5:30, 31 on a large sheet of poster paper, but with key words replaced by blanks as shown.

"The God of our _____ raised _____ from the dead—whom you had _____ by hanging him on a _____. God exalted him to his own right _____ as _____ and _____ that he might give _____ and _____ of sins to _____."

Write the ten missing words on index cards, one word per card. The words, in order, are: *fathers, Jesus, killed, tree, hand, Prince, Savior, repentance, forgiveness, Israel.*

Before students arrive, tape the poster to the wall. Hide the cards in obvious places around the room. Some can be "hidden" on bulletin boards or taped to a wall. Others can go in flowerpots or on shelves.

When you're ready, tell students to pair up to hunt for the index cards. Once they find a card, the pair tries to figure out where their word fits into the passage on the wall. You can ask the class to shout out words as you point to the various blanks.

Once the blanks are filled, discuss the meaning and significance of the passage. Say something like, **This Bible passage shows us a new sort of Passover. The original one involved the blood of lambs and saved the people of Israel from the Egyptians. The new Passover involves the blood of the Son of God, Jesus. In fact, because of this, Jesus is called the Lamb of God. His sacrifice paid the price for our sins once and for all. No more blood of any kind is required. This final Passover saves us forever from our sins.**

If someone asks about Jesus being crucified on a tree, explain that the word in the original language could mean *tree, pole, wooden beam,* or similar object. Be sure everyone understands the meaning of *repentance* and other key words.

Extra-Credit Game: Have your learners decode the word *Passover*. Tell them the code is A = 1, B = 2, C = 3, and so on through the alphabet. Write the coded version, 16 1 19 19 15 22 5 18, on the chalkboard or poster paper.

Conclusion Activity: Distribute Band-Aids, one per student. If they have Bibles, encourage your learners to stick the Band-Aids to the cover or flyleaf. Otherwise, have them stick the bandages to the backs of their hands. Say, **When you see your Band-Aid, remember that your sins have been completely forgiven by the blood of the Lord Jesus. His death paid the price for our sins. Leave the Band-Aids on your hands for a day and on your Bibles forever.**

THE POET'S CORNERED!

And the blood of Jesus, his Son, purifies us from all sin
(1 John 1:7).

Sometimes poetry in a magazine is on a page called "The Poet's Corner." Well, this time you are the poet and we've got you cornered! We've made a poem based on the Bible story you just heard. We left out some key words in the stanzas—you figure out what you think they should be. Naturally, they gotta rhyme!

The Egyptians were blowing it—
They wouldn't let God's people go;
So God told Moses, "I'm going to wipe them out,
And you're the first to _____.

"Put the blood of the lamb on your doorposts—
This will be a sign;
I won't kill those who do as I say,
Because they are all _____."

At midnight it happened,
Just as God had said;
The Israelites were safe at home,
but the Egyptian firstborn were _____.

Remember the Passover story,
Remember Jesus, who was crucified;
He shed his blood to save us,
It's the reason that he _____.

The blood of Jesus purifies us from sin,
It says in 1 John 1:7;
Because he died to pay the price,
We who believe can go to _____.

6. Crossing the Red Sea

Bible Passage: Exodus 14:5-31.
Lesson Theme: God is all-powerful.

STORY

Story Starter: Ask the learners, *What was the greatest feat of strength you've ever seen?* Allow a few kids to answer, then say something like, *I want you to listen to a story about an incredible display of power. It's not the story of someone lifting a great load or pulling a huge weight. Instead, it's a tale of power against power—Almighty God pitted against the strongest army on earth. As you'll hear, God is so strong he was able to completely wipe out the bad guys without touching even one man.*

The story is true. But listen as I read you an imaginary story about an eccentric Egyptian inventor who lived near the Red Sea at the time of Israel's great escape from Egypt.

A delivery chariot pulled up in front of the laboratory of Professor Irving M. Nutcase, and a delivery boy, struggling to haul an awkward, large box, approached the professor's door.

"Special delivery from the Acme Do-It-Yourself Submarine Company for Professor Nutcase," he shouted as he knocked. A wild-eyed man wearing a white lab coat and a black bow tie answered the door. "Sign here, Professor."

"Ah! At last, my package has arrived," exclaimed the white-haired Nutcase. "Now my great scientific genius can be unleashed. At last the world will know that I, Professor Irving M. Nutcase, am the greatest genius of them all. I shall rule the world! They'll all be my slaves! Harrr!"

The delivery boy ran away as fast as he could. Professor Nutcase was, dear listener, totally bonkers. But he had a plan. A totally bonkers plan. A bonkers man with a bonkers plan.

The professor tore into the package and pulled out one large, wooden barrel, two leather bags that could be inflated with air by blowing into a hose, and a propeller. It wasn't much, dear listener, but don't forget—this was ancient Egypt.

"With my submarine and my secret chemical formula, I can dry up all the oceans of the world," the professor shouted to himself. (Mad scientists always shout to themselves, you know.)

"I'll control the seas. Ships will be left high and dry. International trade will come to a halt. I will be in control. I will rule the world! They'll all be my slaves! Harrr!" (The professor tended to repeat himself when he raved.)

"At last, I have the submarine—all I have to do now is invent a chemical that will dry up oceans. Merely a small detail."

And so Professor Nutcase began searching for his formula. During the nights he mixed chemicals in his secret laboratory near the edge of the Red Sea. During the days he tested his formulas in the sea, aboard his leaky, wooden submarine. Despite months of failure, he continued in his mad quest for world domination.

Meanwhile, down in the heart of Egypt, something truly important was happening. (You, dear listener, should understand that this part of our story is the true part.)

Almighty God had commanded Moses to lead the people of Israel out of Egypt, where they had been slaves for centuries. Moses and the Israelites were to head across the desert to a new land that God promised to prepare for them.

Of course, the king of Egypt did not want to lose thousands of slaves. So when Moses and the people marched across the border of Egypt, the king and his army jumped in their chariots and gave chase.

Now Moses was a good man. He obeyed God and strongly believed in God's power and ability. But not so the Israelites. Most of them had little faith in God. In fact, they were big chickens. When the Israelites saw the approaching Egyptian army, they were terrified. They said to Moses, "What have you done to us by bringing us out of Egypt? It would have been better for us to serve the Egyptians than to die in the desert!"

They may have had a point there, except for one fact that had escaped their notice: God was on their side. He would fight for them.

Moses replied, "Do not be afraid. Stand firm and you will see the deliverance the Lord will bring you today. The Egyptians you see today you will never see again. The Lord will fight for you; you need only be still."

Then God spoke to Moses. He told him to raise the staff in his hand over the Red Sea, which was blocking Israel's escape. Moses stretched out his hand, and all that night the Lord drove the sea back with a strong east wind and turned it into dry land.

Now back to the made-up part of our story. When Professor Nutcase, who was aboard his wooden sub trying another chemical compound, saw the dry ground running across the Red Sea, he was ecstatic. "At last! Success! Now the world will know that I, Professor Irving M. Nutcase, am the greatest genius of them all. I shall rule the world! They'll all be my slaves! Harrr!"

Meanwhile, the Israelites were racing across the sea on dry ground. The Egyptians pursued them, and all Pharaoh's horses and chariots and horsemen followed them into the sea. At that point, God threw the Egyptian army into confusion, and he made the wheels of the chariots come off so they had difficulty driving. The Egyptians said, "Let's get away from the Israelites! The Lord is fighting for them against Egypt."

Then the Lord said to Moses, "Stretch out your hand over the sea so that the waters may flow back over the Egyptians and their chariots and horsemen." Moses did as he was told. The waters swept over Pharaoh and his army. Not one soldier survived.

But the Israelites went through the sea on dry ground, with a wall of water on their right and left. That day the Lord saved Israel from the hands of the Egyptians, and Israel saw the Egyptians lying dead on the shore. And when the Israelites saw the great power the Lord displayed, the people were awestruck—they put their trust in him and in Moses his servant. This is how God saved Israel from slavery to Egypt.

And what, dear listeners, about our friend Professor Nutcase? Well, as you might guess, his final words were, "Now the world will (blub) know that I, Professor Irving (blub, blub) M. Nutcase, am the greatest (blub, blub, blub) genius of them all. I shall (blub, choke, splutter) rule the (choke, splutter, blub) world! They'll all be my (blub, blub, blub blub . . .)!"

GAME INSTRUCTIONS

Materials Needed: One photocopy of the game for each pair of players, colored pens or pencils (two different colors for each game sheet), coins.

Approximate Playing Time: 5-10 minutes.

Special Instructions: Try this game before class to be sure you know how it works. Hand out photocopied games. Read the instructions aloud.

TEACHING IDEAS

Materials Needed:

Learning project: one large muscle-man picture for each group of three or four learners, pictures of various heavy objects, paste, typing or construction paper.

Conclusion activity: notebook paper, pencils or pens.

Discussion Starters: What was the big problem the Israelites faced as they left Egypt? How did God overcome this problem? If God can wipe out such a huge problem (the Egyptian army was probably the most powerful on earth at the time), do you think he can handle problems we face? How can we be sure God will come and help us?

Learning Project: Buy one of those muscle-and-brawn magazines. (Or, if you're too embarrassed, make somebody else do it for you.) Cut out a few pictures of muscle men posing or lifting weights. The photos should be as large as possible. You'll need one photo per group of three or four students. Students will also need pictures of buildings, airplanes, elephants, or any other heavy object that can be pasted in the arms of the muscle men. The idea is for students to make posters depicting superhuman feats of strength. Supply each group with pictures, paste, and paper.

Tell your learners what they are to do, and tell them to write something at the top of their posters that describes how God is far stronger than any human on earth. Explain that God was able to defeat the mighty Egyptian army by his powerful miracle of separating the waters of the Red Sea. He can defeat any problem we may face in our own lives.

Allow groups to display and discuss their finished projects.

Conclusion Activity: Have each student work individually to make a prayer list—a list of things to talk to God about. The list can include problems to be dealt with, friends who need God's help, things they need, and praises for the Lord's goodness and power. Encourage all to set a time when they will pray about the things on their lists.

IN OVER OUR HEADS!

The water flowed back and covered the chariots and horsemen—the entire army of Pharaoh that had followed the Israelites into the sea. Not one of them survived. But the Israelites went through the sea on dry ground, with a wall of water on their right and on their left (Exodus 14:28, 29).

The Bible makes it clear that all the Israelites made it safely across and all the Egyptians were drowned. But let's pretend that one Israelite chickened out. He saw the walls of water and started to run back the way he came—toward the Egyptians. Now he's in the middle of the water, drowning. Will he make it safely out? See if you can help him.

You help the man swim to safety by drawing a pencil line from him to the shore. To draw the line, flip a coin. If it's "heads," draw your line one grid space north (starting at the man). If it's "tails," draw the line one grid space west. North and west are marked on the map. By flipping the coin many times, you will draw a line that staggers across the water to the north and west.

As your line wanders, it will probably hit some obstacles. Each time the man hits an obstacle, he gets weaker. If you hit three obstacles, the man drowns. Start over if you like. The obstacles are things like sharks, sharp rocks, and whirlpools. Play with a friend by drawing two lines.

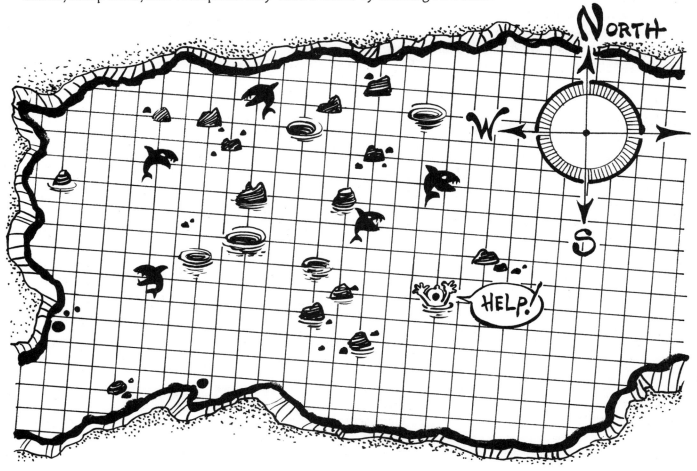

If an Israelite had really gone back, he would have drowned. Why? Because he didn't follow God as he had been told. We must follow God and do as he says, or we will always find ourselves in over our heads.

7. The Golden Calf

Bible Passage: Exodus 32.
Lesson Theme: God wants us to be loyal and faithful to him.

STORY

Story Starter: Ask your students if they like stories or movies about aliens from outer space. Let them tell you the names of their favorite aliens. Say, *No space aliens are ever mentioned in the Bible. But let's pretend that a space alien was visiting earth during an event that the Bible tells us really happened. The alien is filling out a report to send back to his home planet. There is just one problem—this alien misunderstands everything he sees. First, let me read what actually happened. Then I'll read the alien's report.*

God told Moses to lead the children of Israel out of Egypt to the Promised Land. They crossed the Red Sea, where God miraculously parted the waters so all the people could pass over on dry ground. Now they were heading across the desert toward their goal, the country that God had promised to give them. While the Israelites were camped, Moses went up on a mountain to speak to God. He was up there for more than a month, and the people became very restless.

They came to Aaron, Moses' helper, and said, "Come, make us gods who will lead us. As for Moses, we don't know what happened to him."

Aaron told the people to bring their gold earrings. He melted the gold and fashioned a statue of a calf. The people threw a big celebration, worshipping the gold calf with singing and dancing.

Meanwhile, up on the mountain, God was telling Moses what the children of Israel were up to. God was very angry—and so was Moses when he came down the mountain and saw it for himself. Moses burned the calf in the fire, ground it to powder, mixed the powder with water, and made all the people drink it. Sort of like washing your mouth out with soap.

Although he was furious, Moses prayed that God would forgive this sin of rebellion and idolatry. God did, ordering Moses to continue leading the people to the Promised Land. However, many people became sick with a plague.

Now let's look at this same story again through our imaginary space alien's eyes—all three of them.

REPORT 1X-9-0
To: THE GALACTIC DISINTEGRATION COUNCIL
From: SPACE AGENT THUDPUCKER
Regarding: EARTH

My assignment is to examine the intelligent life-forms on planet Earth to determine if Earth should be disintegrated or not. If the life-forms are too intelligent, the planet must be destroyed so there will be no threat to the peace and safety of the galaxy.

Day #1: I have landed undetected in a desert area and have located a large group of humans, the most intelligent species on the planet. They are camped at the base of a mountain. Using my superior technology, I am observing their habits and behavior so that I can determine whether or not they are smart enough to be a danger to our galaxy.

Day #2: The humans have constructed a golden image of a cow (a fat, brainless beast used for food). The humans drink a white fluid that they drain from the animal. They call it milk. Yeeck!

They are throwing some sort of strange celebration centered on the golden cow. The people are carrying the cow all around the camp. People are falling down, some of them apparently intoxicated. Others are throwing flowers at the image. I have no idea why they are doing this: Cows do not consume flowers.

Day #3: A single human has come down from the nearby mountain. He is screaming and yelling at the other humans. I do not know how to read human emotions, so I can only assume he is very happy that the people have made the golden cow.

Now the man has made a huge fire. In what I feel is a misguided attempt to warm the symbolic cow in the fire, he has melted the image to a puddle of gold.

You won't believe what these fools are doing now. They have ground the gold to powder, mixed it with water, and swallowed it. I'd rather drink cow fluid.

Day #4: The people are very sick. I would be too, if I was dumb enough to drink powdered gold.

FINAL RECOMMENDATION TO THE GALACTIC DISINTEGRATION COUNCIL: Earth presents absolutely no danger. These people are idiots!

After the Story: Play the game. Then, to be sure everyone understands the story, ask your students the suggested discussion starters.

GAME INSTRUCTIONS

Materials Needed: One photocopy of the game per player, pencils.

Approximate Playing Time: 5-7 minutes.

Special Instructions: Hand out the games, one to each player. Gather students into groups of two or three to play. As always, read the verse and instructions as players follow along on their game sheets.

After the Game: Discuss the significance of the answer, which is, "No loyalty to God."

TEACHING IDEAS

Materials Needed:

Object lesson: a pet dog or a picture of a dog.

Learning project: construction paper or newsprint, colored pens.

Discussion Starters: Why did the people want Aaron to make gods to worship? Where was Moses and what was he doing there? Our imaginary space alien thought Moses was happy when he saw the golden calf. Was he? The alien thought Moses wanted to warm the calf in the fire. What was he really doing? Why do you think God and Moses were so unhappy about the golden calf? We don't worship golden calves today. We Christians worship God because we know that he is the source of true happiness and salvation. But what are some things that non-Christians think will bring them happiness? Can these things really replace God?

Object Lesson: Show a picture of a dog (or better still, bring in a friendly, well-behaved dog). Say, *This animal is often called man's best friend. What are some things about dogs that make them such good pals?* The main answer you are looking for is *loyalty*. Explain that God wants us to be loyal and faithful to him.

Learning Project: Provide construction paper or newsprint and colored pens for constructing a poster. The poster is to be a contract between the students and God—a commitment to remain loyal to him. The poster can range from a simple statement such as, "We promise to always love the Lord," to a list of things the students promise to do (pray, read the Bible, come to Sunday school, for example). Don't allow your learners to list anything impractical. Let them work on one or more posters, depending on the size of your group.

Conclusion Activity: After discussing the contracts, you and your students should sign them and display them on the wall.

Calf? What Calf?

So Moses went back to the Lord and said, "Oh, what a great sin these people have committed! They have made themselves gods of gold" (Exodus 32:31).

When Moses went up to the mountain to talk with God, the people he left behind decided to make their own gods. They melted down their earrings and formed a golden calf. They wanted to replace the true God with a silly animal.

Why did the people turn away from God? Because they had a big problem. By playing this game, you can find out what the problem was.

Instructions: Each calf at the top of the game is connected by a string to a circle below. Use a pencil to follow each string. Write the letter that appears on each calf in the connected circle—one has been done as an example. If you follow the strings properly, you'll spell out the Israelites' problem.

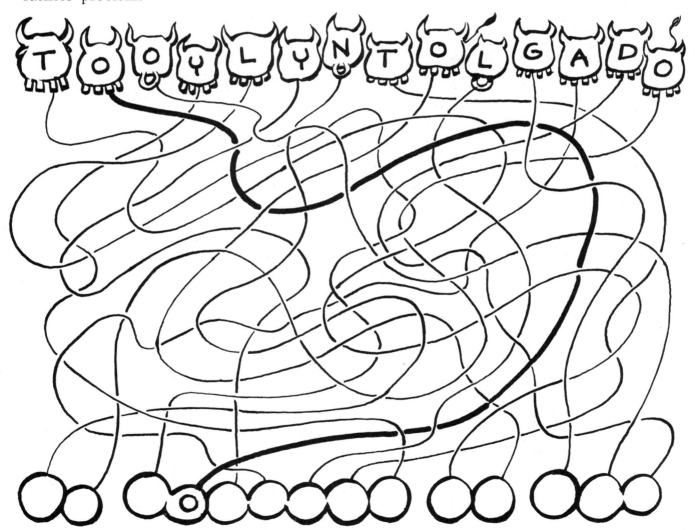

8. The Bronze Snake

> **Bible Passage:** Numbers 21:4-9; John 3:14, 15.
> **Lesson Theme:** In the battle for our souls, God sometimes fights tough.

STORY

Story Starter: This fun guessing game will draw your learners' attention to the story of the poisonous snakes that God sent to discipline the children of Israel.

The object is for your students to guess the word *snake*. You will give several hints, allowing students to hazard one or two guesses after each hint. The hints are sentences in which the word *snake* has been replaced by the word *banana*. Here are the hints.

1. A banana is an animal.
2. Some bananas are dangerous.
3. Dangerous bananas can kill you, but they will never eat you.
4. Bananas crawl in trees and on the ground.
5. Bananas slither.
6. Bananas have fangs and venom.

Tell your students how to play the game, then begin. They will probably guess the answer after the third or fourth clue. Congratulate them, then say, ***I'm going to read a story about snakes. No bananas involved, just snakes.***

"Hi, kids. It's me, your amazingly handsome father, home from work. Whatcha watching?"

Ryan and his sister Megan smiled at each other. They liked their father. He had a weird sense of humor. He was not amazingly handsome. He was, in fact, sort of dumpy looking. But they knew he was the best dad in the world. Or at least on the block.

"Oh, most amazingly handsome Father," sang Megan. "We are watching a box in the corner of the room. It has pictures on it. It's called 'television.'"

"Incredible," Father said. "What will they think of next? I suppose you are filling your brilliant brains with wonderfully educational programming material?" Father said this with a touch of irony, since he knew there was absolutely no chance his two kids would be watching anything of value on television.

"Sure, Dad," Ryan said. "It's great. Lots of violence and blood."

"Looks like we need to have a talk about what you guys watch. What is it? A classic historical film, like *Rambo*?"

"C'mon, Dad. Actually, it's an after-school special about two street gangs in Los Angeles. One gang is called the Snakes and the other is the Desert Rats. They hate each other and beat each other up."

"The Snakes and the Desert Rats, eh? Turn off the TV; this reminds me of a story."

"Oh no. Not another one of your corny stories!" Ryan and Megan groaned good-naturedly. But they turned off the TV without an argument because they knew their dad's stories were always fun to listen to.

"My story is about two gangs way out in the desert," Dad began. "One gang was called the Snakes, just like on TV. The other gang was kind of like the Desert Rats, but they called their gang the Children of Israel."

"The Children of Israel," said Megan knowingly. "Dad, is this a Bible story?"

"Yep. I think you'll like it. I guess I better start at the beginning.

"The Children of Israel—let's call them the Chill for short, 'cause that sounds like a good name for a gang. Anyway, the Chill gang was heading across the desert. They had just escaped from the state penitentiary where they were serving a life sentence of hard labor, breaking rocks."

"I know this story," said Megan with a giggle. "You mean the Israelites had just escaped from Egypt, where they had been slaves. They had to make bricks for the Egyptians. But God told Moses to bring the Israelites out of Egypt to the Promised Land. They had escaped across the Red Sea and were now traveling through the desert, following God to the land he promised to give them."

"Wow, Megan. You're pretty sharp for a kid," Dad teased. Ryan told Megan to shut up so Dad could get on with the story.

"But the Chill gang was upset. A lot of the gang members came to their leader, a dude named Moses, and said, 'Yo, there ain't no hamburger stands in this crummy desert. This stinks!'"

Ryan chimed in. "I remember, Dad. The Israelites spoke against God and against Moses. They complained about the food and the lack of water. They wanted to stop following God and turn back."

"That's right. And this is where the other gang comes in; the Snakes. God sent in the Snakes who . . . "

"Wait, Dad," Megan interrupted. "God sent poisonous snakes to bite the people of Israel. Many of them died. The rest came to Moses and cried out, 'We sinned when we spoke against the Lord and against you. Pray that the Lord will take the snakes away from us.'"

"Have I told you this story before?" Dad asked.

"We heard it in Sunday school," answered Megan.

Ryan continued the story, "The Lord told Moses to make a bronze snake and put it up on a pole. Anyone who was bitten could look at the snake and live. It was like a miracle. But, Dad, why did God do it in such a weird way? Why didn't he just take away the snakes?"

"Let me get my Bible. I want to read something Jesus said."

When he returned with his Bible, Ryan and Megan's dad read John 3:14, 15: "'Just as Moses lifted up the snake in the desert, so the Son of Man must be lifted up, that everyone who believes in him may have eternal life.'

"You see, kids, God fights for the people he loves. He wants us to follow him and love him. The Israelites wanted to turn back from following him, so he had to fight tough. He sent poisonous snakes to kill some of them. He didn't want to do that, but he was willing to fight tough in order to win the battle for their hearts and minds. And he had Moses put a bronze snake on a pole to symbolize what Jesus would do centuries later. Jesus was crucified so that people who believed would be healed from the poison of sin."

"So the bronze snake healed people from the poison of the snakes," mused Megan, "and Jesus heals people from the poison of sin. That's a wonderful story,

Dad. I especially like the part about God fighting tough to win our love. He was willing to send the snakes, even though they would hurt the ones he loved."

"More than that, kids. Much more than that. God was willing to fight so tough for us, that he sent his son Jesus to die on the cross. That's fighting tough. That's how much God loves you and me."

GAME INSTRUCTIONS

Materials Needed: One photocopy of the game per player, pencils.

Approximate Playing Time: 2-3 minutes.

Special Instructions: Hand out a photocopied game to each player. Players should work together in pairs. Be sure everyone understands the instructions. Allow all groups to finish before revealing the solution.

TEACHING IDEAS

Discussion Starters: Where was God leading the children of Israel? What did they start complaining about? Why do you think it was so wrong for them to complain? What did God tell Moses to do? How was the bronze snake a symbol of Jesus? Why did Jesus have to die for us?

Learning Project: There are two steps to this activity.

The first step is a "crowd breaker," an activity that lets the children interact. Before class, copy John 3:14, 15 onto a sheet of paper as shown in the illustration.

Photocopy and cut up as many verses as you need for each student to receive one section of the passage. Do not reveal what the completed passage says until the game is over. At your signal, students attempt to find others with the pieces that successfully complete the passage. Depending on the number of participants, there may be one or two students who cannot complete the passage.

Discuss the passage, explaining how it connects to the story of the snakes. At the end of the passage, Jesus stresses that anyone who believes in him will receive eternal life.

The second step of the project introduces the concept of eternity. Ask several of the learners to solve the following problems (and any additional problems you dream up) on a calculator or chalkboard. Tell them, **As torture, you have to wash one million dinner dishes. If you could wash, dry, and put away one dish per minute, about how many years would it take to complete the job? At your job you earn $5 an hour. About how many centuries would you have to work, day and night, to buy Greenland if it was for sale for one billion dollars?**

Tell your learners that these large numbers don't even add up to the first day of the infinite number of years we'll spend in heaven if we believe in Jesus.

Conclusion Activity: Have small groups draw a cartoon of a bottle of "Spiritual Poison Antidote." The label should explain that sin is the poison and that Jesus is the cure. The students can also describe how the antidote is to be applied (how to become a Christian).

Snakebit!

The people came to Moses and said, "We sinned when we spoke against the Lord and against you. Pray that the Lord will take the snakes away from us." So Moses prayed for the people. The Lord said to Moses, "Make a snake and put it up on a pole; anyone who is bitten can look at it and live" (Numbers 21:7, 8).

To help you remember the story of Moses and the snakes, and the way Jesus' death on the cross was symbolized by the snake on the pole, try this challenging maze.

The object is to go from the starting area to the cross. Along the way, however, there are a lot of snakes. As you move along the paths, you can run across as many as four snakes. But if you hit more than four, you lose—you're snakebit!

9. Balaam's Donkey

Bible Passage: Numbers 22:21-35.
Lesson Theme: God speaks to us in the Bible.

STORY

Story Starter: If you intend to play the Extra-Credit Game, tell your students to listen especially closely to the story because you will give them small prizes if they can answer questions about what they hear. Say, ***This is a story about a Hollywood talent scout who is interviewing a great new talent he has discovered. The scout is hoping to cast her in a new television show. She is with her agent, a man named Mr. Balaam. Let's listen in as they talk.***

(This story comes across best if you use distinctly different voices for the talent scout, the agent, and the donkey. Since identifying the speakers is cumbersome in this story, voice changes alone cue the listeners to who's talking.)

"Baby, sweetie, doll face. We're going to make a star out of you. You're fresh, you're new, you're hip."

"Thanks, Mr. Wheeler."

"I wasn't talking about you, Balaam. I meant your girl here."

"Oh, sorry."

"I sure appreciate you giving me this chance. I've always wanted to come to Hollywood and be on TV. It's so exciting," she breathed.

"I know it is, doll. All the kids want to come here and be big stars. Most of them don't stand a chance. But you, you're different. You've got that certain something that sets you apart from all the animals out there."

"Now listen here, Wheeler, my girl may be fresh and young, but she's no dummy. Let's get down to business. Show us a contract."

"Keep your shirt on, Balaam. First, I got to get her story. For the press releases, you know? The fans will want to know all about this little filly. I tell you, she's gonna to be big, big, big!"

"Well, let me tell you how I came to be her agent. It's an interesting story. As you know, I used to be a prophet. A prophet is someone who is supposed to tell people what God wants to say to them. But I didn't work for Almighty God. I worked for all the pagan gods and idols worshipped by the countries surrounding Israel.

"One day I was summoned by the king of Moab. He promised me a lot of money if I would put a curse on Israel. That night, Almighty God—the God of Israel— appeared to me and told me not to do it. But eventually I decided to ignore him, take the money, and go curse Israel. So I saddled up my donkey and headed down the trail.

"On the way, an angel from God stood in the path with a drawn sword in his hand. I couldn't see the angel, but my donkey could. Naturally, the animal was scared, so she jumped off the path into a field. Since I couldn't see the angel, I beat the animal.

"Farther ahead we came to a narrow part of the trail between two walls. Again the angel appeared to my donkey, and again he was invisible to me. The donkey squashed my foot against the wall, so I hit her again.

"This happened a third time. The angel appeared to the donkey. She sat down and wouldn't move. Well, by then I was furious, so I hit the donkey again and again, as hard as I could. The angel then did a miracle. He opened the donkey's mouth so she could talk to me! She said, 'What have I done to you to make you beat me these three times?'

"Well, after I picked my jaw up off the dirt, I got into an argument with my donkey. I accused her of making a fool of me, and she said she had always been a good donkey.

"At this point the Lord opened my eyes so I could see the angel. After I picked my eyeballs up off the dirt, I spoke with the angel. He told me I was sinning by disobeying God. God had told me not to curse Israel; but since I wouldn't listen to him, perhaps I would listen to a donkey. In fact, although the angel didn't say so, I think he was suggesting that my donkey was smarter than I am."

"That's an interesting story, Mr. Balaam. And that's when you first became aware of your client's talent?"

"Yes."

"Well, you were certainly smart to come to me. Your talking donkey is going to be the biggest thing since Mr. Ed, the talking horse. What do you say to that, little lady?"

"Hee haw! Hee haw!"

GAME INSTRUCTIONS

Materials Needed: One photocopy of the game per player, pencils, scissors, paste, thin black cardboard, a wall mirror.

Approximate Playing Time: 10 minutes.

Special Instructions: This game is more like a project that will capture your students' imaginations and help them remember the story of Balaam's donkey. Let each student work on a copy of the project; have students help each other in small groups.

After the Game: Allow students to keep the animation circles. Talk through Discussion Starters, then do the Object Lesson.

TEACHING IDEAS

Materials Needed:

Object lesson: cookbook, Bible.

Extra-credit game: trash can, masking tape, marshmallows, ten story questions.

Conclusion activity: prepared membership cards, or pens and index cards.

Discussion Starters: If a donkey spoke to you, would you stop and listen? Why? If an angel appeared to you and said, "I have a special message to you from Almighty God," would you pay attention? Would you do what the angel instructed you to do? Why? Does God usually talk to people through angels or donkeys? What has God given to us that tells us all about him and lets us know how he wants us to live? Why do you suppose it's important to read the Bible?

Object Lesson: Show your learners a cookbook. Say, *This is a cookbook. What is a cookbook for? Right. It tells us how to cook. It contains recipes that show us how to put food and seasonings together to make good tasting, nourishing meals.*

Now show a Bible. Explain that the Bible is very much like a cookbook. It contains God's recipes for life. It tells us all about God and how he wants us to live. The Bible is the only thing we need in order to learn what God wants to tell us. We don't need any donkeys.

Extra-Credit Game: Set a trash can several feet from a masking tape foul line on the floor. Kids attempt to throw marshmallows (or any small objects) into the can. Tell players the name of the game is "Feed the Donkey." Anyone who hits the target wins a piece of candy or other prize. Anyone who misses is asked a question about the story. Players who can answer the questions win a prize. Each player gets one throw per turn. Prepare eight or ten questions in advance. It's good to ask a question more than once; this reinforces the answer.

Conclusion Activity: The illustration on this page can be used to make membership cards in The Talking Donkey Club. Photocopy enough for each student to have one. Alternately, you can allow students to draw their own.

Read James 1:22-25. You can paraphrase the passage and say something like, *Some people read the Bible, but don't obey what it says. They are like a person who looks in the mirror when he wakes up, sees that he needs to brush his teeth, wipe his nose, and comb his hair—but does nothing. But the person who looks in the Bible and responds to what he sees, that person is blessed by God.*

Tell students, *I have an idea. I think we should form a club. We'll call it "The Talking Donkey Club." Anyone who belongs to this club promises to obey the Bible. Take the cards I've given you and write something like, "I promise to always obey what God tells me to do in the Bible." Then sign your name and the date.*

Encourage your learners to keep the cards in their Bibles, purses, or wallets, or to post them on their bedroom walls. The animation circles can also be posted on the wall.

Follow Up: If membership in The Talking Donkey Club seems to excite your learners, take advantage of the opportunity to give them Bible commands to read and obey. In future Bible studies, copy some of the commands and give them to club members to post and memorize. You could make a system of points with simple prizes. The Bible commands could be printed up in a club newsletter.

Honkin' Donkeys!

Then the Lord opened the donkey's mouth, and she said to Balaam, "What have I done to you to make you beat me these three times?" (Numbers 22:28).

Now there's an unusual miracle. A talking donkey! Just for fun, we thought you'd like to try a little project. Here's what to do.

1.   Paste this page to a sheet of black cardboard. It's very important that the back of the cardboard is black. Cut out the wheel, including all the slots. Stick a pencil through the center as shown.

2.   The drawing shows how to look through the slots into a mirror as you spin the wheel. With a little practice, you'll see the donkey talking!

10. Achan Steals Some Goodies

Bible Passage: Joshua 7.
Lesson Theme: Things that can distract us from God.

STORY

Story Starter: See the Object Lesson for an interesting way to start this story. Read the story as if you were a tough-talking private investigator.

 ❖ ❖ ❖

It was 8:00 a.m. on a Monday. I was in my crummy office down in the dusty part of town. Me? I'm Mike Nail, Private Investigator. I'm the best money can buy. Except not too many people buy me, so I have this crummy office down in the dusty part of town.

I was sitting there eating leftover pizza and drinking coffee, black, from my old beat-up Ninja Turtle thermos bottle, when the chief of police walked in the door.

"Mike," he said, "there's been a robbery. The crime was reported by Joshua, the leader of the children of Israel. A beautiful robe, 200 shekels of silver, and a large bar of gold have been stolen from the city of Jericho."

"Jericho, eh? I've heard of that place. The walls fell down when the children of Israel marched around it. Then Joshua and his people burned the city. They took all the silver and gold and other valuable items to put in the treasury of the Lord, just as God had told them."

"That's right, Mike. But when Israel went to make war against the next town, a place called Ai, the people there were able to beat up the Israelites pretty badly. That's when Joshua realized something was wrong, and he came right to me. I didn't mention this to Joshua, but the way I figure it, someone disobeyed God by keeping some of the loot from Jericho, and that's why God didn't fight for Israel at Ai."

"Gotcha, Chief. And now you've come to me to bail you out because you and your boys are stumped."

"It's a tough case, Mike. There are no fingerprints at the scene of the crime. No clues at all. Nothing. As near as I can tell, if there is a crook, he got away clean."

That afternoon, I jumped on my classic '57 camel and drove over to Jericho. The chief had been right. No evidence. Still, I couldn't shake the eerie feeling that, somehow, there would be a break in the case. The little voice in my head was telling me to have a talk with Joshua. I cameled over to the Israelite camp and knocked on his tent flap. Since knocking on tent flaps doesn't make any sound, I let myself in.

Inside, a man was on his knees. It was Joshua, talking to God. I listened in.

"O Lord, what can I say, now that Israel has been routed by its enemies? The Canaanites and the other people of the country will hear about this and they will surround us and wipe out our name from the earth. What then will you do for your own great name?"

Then I heard the Lord say to Joshua, "Stand up! What are you doing down on your face? Israel has sinned. They have taken some of the things devoted to my treasury. They have stolen, they have lied. That is why the Israelites cannot stand against their enemies."

As I continued to listen, God told Joshua to get all the people together the following day. I crept away and went to my favorite grill for a steak burger and fries. Then I went down the street for a pizza. After that, some ice cream with chocolate sauce. Then it was time to head for home. For some reason, my camel seemed to have a hard time making it up the hills.

Tuesday came. I was there and so was Joshua and all the people of Israel. God told Joshua to cast lots. That's kind of like drawing the short straw or pulling your name from a hat. In this case, the lots were cast and the first lot went to the tribe of Judah. So we knew that the crook belonged to the tribe called Judah. But that was still tens of thousands of people. So another lot was cast. The lot went to the clan of the Zerahites. The next lot took the family of Zimri. Each family member came forward one by one, and the lot fell to a man named Achan. A fitting name; he looked like he was aching to me.

Achan spilled his guts like a bag of coffee beans with a hole in it. He confessed to the whole thing. He admitted that when he saw the plunder in Jericho, he couldn't resist taking some of the things that belonged to God. He took them and hid them for fear of discovery.

Joshua sent some guys to dig up the loot. They found it, just where Achan said it would be. Unhappily for Achan, he was punished to the full extent of the law. He was stoned to death. Tough break, kid.

And me? Well, the chief thinks I was the one who solved the case. He gave me a medal and a new thermos bottle. I didn't tell him it was really God who revealed the guilty party. I'll never tell.

GAME INSTRUCTIONS

Materials Needed: One photocopy of the game for each player, pencils, red cloth.

Approximate Playing Time: 8-10 minutes.

Special Instructions: Younger children may find the game difficult. You can help them two ways. First, fill in a few of the words before photocopying the game. (See the solution at the end of the book.) Then as children play the game, walk around offering help and encouragement.

Lead into the game by waving a red cloth in front of your learners. Ask, *Can you think of an animal that might be strongly attracted to this waving red cloth? Bulls are supposedly attracted by red. Matadors usually use red capes to make the bull charge. The cape hides the knife the matador uses to kill the unfortunate animal. The red cape distracts the bull from the blade.*

Unhappily, there are things in life that can distract our attention from God. As Christians, we are supposed to love our Lord and pay attention to him. He is to be most im-

portant in our lives. But the world contains many distractions. Let's take a look at some.

When ready to play, assemble students into groups of two or three. Hand out games. As always, read aloud the game's Scripture passage, as well as the instructions for playing.

After the Game: Go over the solution at the end of the book. (The word *kicks* is slang, meaning to build one's life on frivolous things while excluding God.) Discuss some of the things that can detour a person from God. Some of them are obvious, such as drugs or gold (love of money). Some are less obvious. Doing homework, for example, is a good thing and something that God wants us to do well. But a person who doesn't do the homework on time may have to skip an important church activity or Bible study to get it done.

We suggest you take a moment to not only tell about a time when something distracted you from God, but also tell what decisions you had to make because you were distracted.

TEACHING IDEAS

Materials Needed:

Object lesson: a silly mask or costume, confetti or small candies.

Learning project: crayons, colored pens, newsprint, masking tape, chalkboard or poster paper for phrases.

Discussion Starters: What was Joshua, the leader of Israel, supposed to do with all the riches of the city of Jericho? What did Achan do wrong? Why do you suppose he wanted the stuff? Achan was willing to disobey God in order to take some of the things he wanted. Name some things that we must have in order to stay alive and healthy. Do we have to disobey God to have these things? Can God provide the things we need?

Object Lesson: Arrange beforehand for an adult to bring a mask or silly costume. Begin to read the story. When you are two or three sentences into it, the costumed adult bursts into the room shouting something ridiculous like, "I saw the ghost of Elvis Presley!" The adult should run about the room tossing confetti or small candies, then suddenly leave.

At this point, your students will be thoroughly distracted from the story. Tell them that the theme of the lesson is distractions and that you planned the little interruption as an example of distraction in action. Start

the story again, encouraging students to figure out who in the story was distracted, what he was distracted by, and who or what he was distracted from.

Learning Project: Supply crayons or colored pens and newsprint to groups of three or four students so they can make a fanciful map. List these phrases on a chalkboard or poster for all to see: pray, read the Bible, think about God, attend church service, come to fun youth group events, talk to parents about God, have Christian friends. Add any other things that help a person grow spiritually.

Explain, *Draw an interesting, colorful map that shows the best route to knowing God better. Here's how: Draw a road marked by all of the things I've listed on the board. They can look like road signs or bridges or speed-limit signs. If a person does all these things regularly, he or she will grow closer to God. Put God at the end of the road. I also want you to put detours on your map, things that will distract a person from God. These can be drug abuse, too much television, or anything else you can think of. The game we played listed other distractions. Have fun with your map.*

Display the maps in your room. Discuss some of the detours students include on their maps.

Distractions, Distractions

Achan replied, "It is true! I have sinned against the Lord, the God of Israel. This is what I have done: When I saw in the plunder a beautiful robe from Babylonia, two hundred shekels of silver and a wedge of gold weighing fifty shekels, I coveted them and took them. They are hidden in the ground inside my tent, with the silver underneath" (Joshua 7:20, 21).

Because Achan went after all those things instead of God, he lost everything. There are many things today that can detour us from God. Television is a great example: how many people have stayed home to watch a football game rather than joining friends for the Sunday worship?

On this page is a list of things that might cause us to stumble as we follow the Lord. Some are good, some are very bad—but all can cause us to lose interest in God if we become too interested or involved in them. Your job is to fit all the words into the grid. As in a crossword puzzle, the words must correctly share letters. The hard part? It's up to you to figure out where the words go. We put in a word to help you get started.

Sample game:

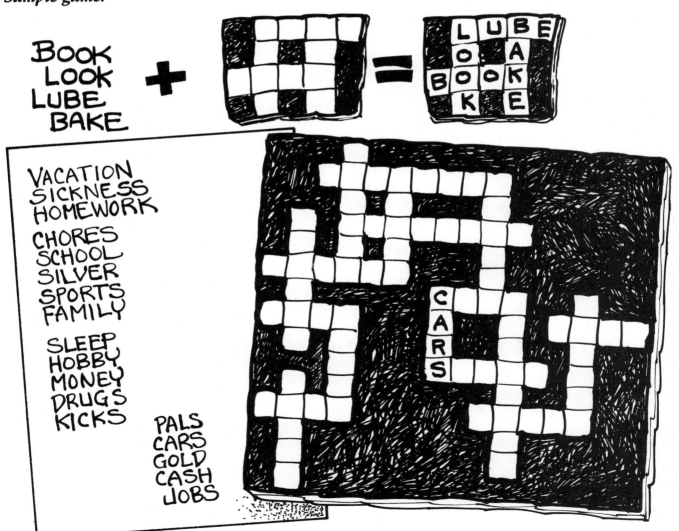

11. Elijah Versus the Prophets of Baal

> **Bible Passage:** 1 Kings 18:17-39.
> **Lesson Theme**: God responds to our needs.

STORY

Story Starter: Ask students who have dogs to tell their dogs' names, any special tricks they can do, any funny things they did, and so on. Say something like, *One of the things about dogs that makes me laugh is the way they beg for food. Some dogs sit and whine, others roll over or do other tricks, some push their dog dishes with their noses. Right now, I want you to put your imaginations in gear. Let's pretend that we are the dog in this story.*

"Boy, am I hungry," Sam the dog said to himself. "I wonder what time it is?" Sam was kind of squat and brown, about the size and shape of a football. With his very short legs, Sam looked like a football on casters. Food was his sole pleasure in life. Exercise was of no interest to Sam.

Sam loved his masters, and he especially loved the kind of food they ate. If he was lucky, he could sometimes score leftover spaghetti, a cookie or two, or a bowl of soggy Froot Loops. Forming the image of these delectable treats in his little doggie brain, Sam decided it was time to alert his masters to his nutritional needs.

Mrs. Clark was in the bedroom with her daughter, Karen. They were sitting on Karen's bed, reading from the Bible. Sam came into the room and sat down on the floor, mentally preparing himself for his food-alert routine.

Mrs. Clark was reading the story of the Old Testament prophet Elijah and 450 prophets of the pagan god Baal. It seems the children of Israel had fallen into the evil practice of idolatry. Sometimes they worshipped the true God, and sometimes they worshipped the false god Baal. This infuriated the righteous Elijah. As Mrs. Clark read, Sam began the first stage of his food-alert routine. He looked her in the face, a dewy expression in his eyes. Mrs. Clark kept on with the story.

Elijah went before the people and said, "How long will you waver between two opinions? If the Lord is God, follow him; but if Baal is God, follow him." But the people said nothing.

Then Elijah said to them, "I am the only one of the Lord's prophets left, but Baal has 450 prophets. Get two bulls for us. Let them chose one for themselves, and let them cut it into pieces and put it on the wood but not set fire to it. I will prepare the other bull and put it on the wood but not set fire to it. Then you call on the name of your god, and I will call on the name of the Lord. The god who answers by fire—he is God."

Then all the people said, "What you say is good."

Elijah said to the prophets of Baal, "Choose one of the bulls and prepare it first, since there are so many of you. Call on the name of your god, but do not light the fire." So they took the bull given them and prepared it.

Then they called on the name of Baal from morning till noon. "O Baal, answer us!" they shouted. But there was no response; no one answered.

"No one is responding to the dog, either," Sam realized. The first part of his routine wasn't working. The soulful look hadn't attracted any notice. So Sam began phase two—tail wagging. Meanwhile, Mrs. Clark continued reading.

But there was no response, no one answered. And the 450 prophets of Baal danced around the altar they had made.

Sam was dancing himself. He wagged and wagged and wagged, jumping about in tiny circles. But Mrs. Clark and Karen were absorbed in the story.

At noon Elijah began to taunt the prophets of Baal. "Shout louder!" he said. "Surely he is a god! Perhaps he is deep in thought, or busy, or traveling. Maybe he is sleeping and must be awakened."

Sam whined, but there was no response. He was becoming desperate. What else could he do? Was there any other trick he could try?

The prophets of Baal shouted louder and slashed themselves with swords and spears, as was their custom, until their blood flowed.

Sam said to himself, "They slashed themselves until their blood flowed? Maybe I could find a pocket knife and . . . naaah."

Midday passed, and they continued their frantic prophesying until the time for the evening sacrifice. But there was no response, no one answered, no one paid attention.

"That's so gross, Mom," said Karen. "Why did those people cut themselves open like that?"

"They thought that Baal would answer their prayers if they did," Mrs. Clark replied.

"But that's stupid, Mom. We don't have to pray like that. All we have to do is simply tell God our needs and he takes care of us."

"Yes, honey. And do you know what happened next in the story? Elijah poured water all over his dead bull so that everyone would know he couldn't light the wood through some trick. Then, with no dancing, no shouting, no slicing, he simply said two sentences: 'O Lord, God of Abraham, Isaac and Israel, let it be known today that you are God in Israel and that I am your servant and have done all these things at your command. Answer me, O Lord, answer me, so these people will know that you, O Lord, are God, and that you are turning their hearts back again.'

"Immediately the fire of the Lord fell and burned up the bull, the wood, the stones, and even the dirt and all the water. And do you know what happened next, Karen? The people fell flat on their faces and cried, 'The Lord—he is God! The Lord—he is God!' And for us today, all we have to do is trust in God and he takes care of us. We don't have to whine and beg like the silly prophets of Baal."

"And we don't have to whine and beg like our silly dog!" said Karen as she gave Sam a big hug. "C'mon, Sam. It's dinnertime."

Sam quietly and happily followed Karen to the kitchen.

GAME INSTRUCTIONS

Materials Needed: One photocopy of the game per player, pencils.

Approximate Playing Time: 3-5 minutes.

Special Instructions: Players can work in groups of two or three.

After the Game: Go over the solution to the game (Baal and the bull both got this. What is it? *Burned*). Describe how Baal was "burned" because the people saw for themselves that he was just a lie.

TEACHING IDEAS

Discussion Starters: Who was Baal? Who was Elijah? Why did Elijah challenge the prophets of Baal? Why did Baal lose the challenge? Why did the Lord win? What was the people's response to the Lord's victory? Since God is real, how should we respond to him today?

Object Lesson: Show your car keys to the class. Tell them, *This ignition key starts the engine. With the power of the engine, I can barrel down the highway many miles an hour. The key unleashes the power. Without the key, I get to push my car. I think I might be able to muscle it across the parking lot, then I'd probably collapse!*

Today I want us to learn about some simple keys that we can use to open God's great power to us. God has the power to energize our lives; we must decide we want to take advantage of that power.

Learning Project: The Extra-Credit Game lists several things that believers of any age do to maintain a healthy relationship with the Lord. Have students work on one of the following ideas:

1.   Have each group make a poster featuring one of the Extra-Credit Game suggestions. Display the posters in a row.

2.   Work with your class to make a wall chart. The chart features all the suggestions as headings, with space to write underneath. The kids make their own small copies of the chart and fill in specific dates and times they will do these things this week. For example, under the heading TALK TO GOD, a student could write, "Every morning this week when I wake up."

3.   Before class, write each suggestion on a separate piece of paper. Tie or tape string to each sheet. The string should be many feet long, enough to snake throughout the room, out the door, and into other areas. Crisscross the strings over and under each other several times. You can do this by winding them around chairs, taping them to the walls and floor, tying them to doorknobs, and so forth. Each group traces the path of one string to find the suggestion at the other end.

Extra-Credit Game: Scramble the following phrases, lettering each scrambled phrase on a card. Give one card to each small group of students. The phrases are: *talk to God, read your Bible, obey the Lord, have Christian friends, come to church.* Add any you like.

Conclusion Activity: Give students gift-wrapping ribbon to tie around their fingers for a short time as a reminder to love God. When they remove the ribbon, they can tie it in a bow on their bedroom doorknobs.

ONE HOT TIME

*When all the people saw this, they fell prostrate and cried,
"The Lord—he is God! The Lord—he is God!"
(1 Kings 18:39).*

It was the battle of the giants—the phony god Baal versus the one true Almighty God. God won the contest with an incredible show of power. Baal didn't show at all. How could he? He didn't exist!

Naturally, the 450 prophets of Baal weren't too happy with the outcome. If you use a pencil or pen to shade in all the prophets with frowns on their faces, you will be able to answer this question:

Baal and the bull both got this. What is it?

12. The Fiery Furnace Incident

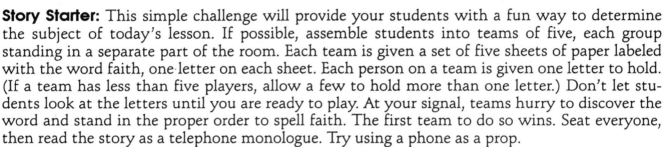

Bible Passage: Daniel 3.
Lesson Theme: The value of strong faith in God.

STORY

Story Starter: This simple challenge will provide your students with a fun way to determine the subject of today's lesson. If possible, assemble students into teams of five, each group standing in a separate part of the room. Each team is given a set of five sheets of paper labeled with the word faith, one letter on each sheet. Each person on a team is given one letter to hold. (If a team has less than five players, allow a few to hold more than one letter.) Don't let students look at the letters until you are ready to play. At your signal, teams hurry to discover the word and stand in the proper order to spell faith. The first team to do so wins. Seat everyone, then read the story as a telephone monologue. Try using a phone as a prop.

This is the story of Shadrach, Meshach, and Abednego, three young men who were thrown into a fiery furnace as punishment for their unyielding faith in Almighty God. They were tossed in by their outraged king, Nebuchadnezzar. But something amazing happened. Let's listen in on an imaginary telephone conversation that took place not long after what we call The Fiery Furnace Incident.

P = PAUSE
SP = SHORT PAUSE

"Hello. Thank you for calling Acme Furnace Repair. This is Fred speaking.ᴾ Who did you say is calling? King Nebuchadnezzar? _The_ King Nebuchadnezzar? Yes, Your Majesty! How can we serve you, Your Majesty?ᴾ

"Your furnace is on the fritz? That's our specialty. Can you describe the furnace to me, Sire?ᴾ It's a four-man furnace? You mean it takes four men to carry?ᴾ No, you mean it holds four men. I see.

"Perhaps if you described the problem to me. I assume it doesn't heat up.ᴾ What? You say it does heat up? I'm afraid I don't understand, Your Majesty. Maybe you better start from the beginning.ᴾ

"You set up a golden statue out in the country. Then you invited all the governors and important officials of the nation to come and worship the statue. Oh, I get it. If the officials would pledge allegiance to your god, that was the same as pledging allegiance to you.ᴾ

"And you had a band there. A musical band. With horns, flutes, lyres, harps, and pipes? Zithers too, eh?ᴾ No, Sire, I don't have any idea what a zither is.ᴾ

"So when all the officials were there, you told them to fall down and worship the statue as soon as the band started to play. Well, this certainly sounds like quite a party, Sire. But, Sire, I'm interested in the furnace.ᴾ Oh, sorry.ᴾ

"You told them what? That if anyone did not fall down and worship the statue you would have them thrown into a fiery furnace. Well, that would sure be an interesting party game, Your Majesty. Hee, hee. Oh, I'm sorry, Sire. No, I'm sure this isn't funny. Go ahead, Sire.

"So the band played and everyone fell down and worshipped the statue. Everyone except three young guys who refused to worship a false god. Wow, Sire. So you had them brought to you. You gave them one more chance. I see. What did they say?

"They said, 'O Nebuchadnezzar, we do not need to defend ourselves before you in this matter. If we are thrown into the blazing furnace, the God we serve is able to save us from it, and he will rescue us from your hand, O king. But even if he does not, we want you to know, O king, that we will not serve your gods or worship the image of gold you have set up.'

"They sound very brave, Sire. What? Did I say brave? Oh no, Your Majesty. I said foolish. They were foolish, stupid, and dumb to oppose you.

"I suppose that's when you tossed them in the furnace. Ah, the soldiers threw them in. And all the soldiers were killed because you had ordered the furnace to be made seven times hotter than usual? Wow. That must have been some marshmallow roast.

"But Your Majesty, there's one thing I don't understand. If the soldiers and the three guys were burned up, if the furnace was seven times hotter than normal, just why have you called Acme Furnace Repair? It sounds to me like you have a pretty good furnace there.

"You say the three guys weren't burned up? You say they walked around inside the flames? And you saw them talking to a *fourth* person inside the flames? You say this fourth person looked like a son of the gods? No, I must say I've never heard of a furnace doing anything like that, Your Lordship. What happened next?

"The three young men came out of the fire. They were completely unharmed. Their hair was not even singed. Not even the smell of smoke was on them. Well, yes, I do see your problem, Sire. I'll do my best to find and fix the problem, Your Majesty. What's that? You say if I don't find the problem I'll be tossed in the furnace? Uh, yes, Sire. I understand. Yes, you have a good day too, Sire. Good-bye."

King Nebuchadnezzar never really called a furnace repair shop. The Bible tells us that King Nebuchadnezzar was furious when Shadrach, Meshach, and Abednego refused to worship and serve his gods. But when God—the true God—saved them in the furnace (in front of hundreds of witnesses), Nebuchadnezzar had a change of heart. Listen to what he said.

Praise be to the God of Shadrach, Meshach and Abednego, who has sent his angel and rescued his servants! They trusted in him and defied the king's command and were willing to give up their lives rather than serve or worship any god except their own God. Therefore I decree that the people of any nation or language who say anything against the God of Shadrach, Meshach and Abednego be cut into pieces and their houses be turned into piles of rubble, for no other god can save in this way (Daniel 3:28, 29).

Then King Nebuchadnezzar promoted the three believers to positions of great importance.

GAME INSTRUCTIONS

Materials Needed: One photocopy of the game per player, pencils.

Approximate Playing Time: 2-3 minutes.

Special Instructions: Hand out games to all players. Allow students to play in pairs.

After the Game: The answer the learners will discover is the face of the devil. Ask students to explain in what sense the devil was "burned" when Shadrach, Meshach, and Abednego remained strongly faithful and obedient to God.

TEACHING IDEAS

Materials Needed:

Object lesson: spool of sewing thread, scissors.

Learning project: ink pad and paper for each group of two or three students, pens, drawing paper.

Conclusion activity: one stamped postcard for each learner.

Discussion Starters: Why did Nebuchadnezzar want his government officials to worship the golden statue? Why do you think Shadrach, Meshach, and Abednego were willing to die for their faith? Who do you think was the fourth person in the flames? It may have been Jesus in the fire, or at least an angel sent by God. We might not be thrown into a furnace nowadays, but people do have trials and troubles, don't they? What are some troubles Jesus can help us with, and how can he help? Can you think of some way he's helped you?

Object Lesson: Show a spool of sewing thread to your class. Say, *How many of you think you can break this thread with your bare hands?* Ask a volunteer to come forward. Have the person extend his or her arms forward with the wrists held together (as if handcuffed). Wrap many turns around the person's wrist, enough to be impossible to break. Let the student struggle for a while, then cut the thread with scissors.

Point out that faith is like the thread. It doesn't seem strong or important, but enough of it can tie a person very tightly to God, just as Shadrach, Meshach, and Abednego were closely bound to their Lord. Say, *Faith is an extremely important part of our relationship with God. We must develop a strong faith in him.*

Learning Project: Give each group of two or three students an ink pad and paper. Each group is to create a comic strip on the paper with thumbprints. Students can draw faces, arms, and legs on the thumbprints to form cartoon characters. Dialogue can be added in cartoon balloons. Each group is free to choose the story, as long as it communicates something about faith. For example, students may illustrate the story of Shadrach, Meshach, and Abednego, or make a mini-poster explaining why the students believe in God.

Conclusion Activity: Read and discuss the last part of Mark 10:27: "All things are possible with God." Provide a stamped postcard for each learner. Say, *Write your name and address on the postcard. On the message area, in big letters, write, "All things are possible with God." I will collect these cards and mail them to you tomorrow. When you get your card, read it and remember the things we spoke of today.*

Dots the Truth, Pal!

"Therefore I decree that the people of any nation or language who say anything against the God of Shadrach, Meshach and Abednego be cut into pieces and their houses be turned into piles of rubble, for no other god can save in this way" (Daniel 3:29).

When Shadrach, Meshach, and Abednego refused to worship the image of gold or serve false gods, the king had them thrown into a blazing furnace. But the king saw a fourth person in the flames with them—a person who sounds a lot like Jesus, if you ask me. What happened to these people? Were any of them burned? Nope. Not even singed. But someone got burned in that furnace. Can you guess who? Connect the dots to find the answer.

13. Jesus Heals a Paralyzed Man

Bible Passage: Mark 2:1-12.
Lesson Theme: Jesus has the power to heal and forgive sins.

STORY

Story Starter: Tell your students, *The story I'm about to read is from the viewpoint of an imaginary Pharisee watching a true incident in Jesus' life. A Pharisee was a religious leader and teacher, highly respected by the people of Israel. Though many Pharisees came to believe in Jesus Christ, most did not. They were jealous of the Lord's popularity with the crowds of people. Because of their actions, Jesus was eventually crucified. Here's how one Pharisee reacted to Jesus.*

I hear that Jesus is at his home in Capernaum. I know that many people will come to hear his words. Who is this Jesus, this man who sways the crowds? I've heard he performs miracles, that he heals the sick and casts out evil spirits, but I do not believe.

I arrive at his home. There are so many people that there is no longer any room indoors. The crowd surrounds the house, peeking in the windows and doorways. I am a Pharisee, deserving of honor, so I make my way inside, near to where Jesus sits. I command a man to move outside and he goes. Those close by make room for me.

Jesus is speaking. I plan to listen very closely. If I can trap him in some wrong teaching, something contrary to Scripture, then I can discredit him, and he will be a problem no longer. I wait.

As Jesus speaks, I notice some dust in the air. It's drifting down from the ceiling. Small pebbles are falling from the ceiling, landing at Jesus' feet. What's happening?

There's a hole in the ceiling! A shaft of sunlight bursts through into the room, dazzling my eyes. The hole is getting bigger. I can see now; someone is up on the flat roof, digging through into the room. Some fools are trying to break through!

Jesus is aware of the commotion. He waits patiently as four men widen the hole. When it is large enough, they lower a man lying on a mat. This is astonishing. Never before have I seen such audacity. These rude men have interrupted our meeting. They must be dealt with firmly. I'll see now how Jesus handles these imbeciles. Perhaps he'll lose his temper.

The man on the mat is paralyzed. He has been brought to Jesus to be healed. Oh, this is wonderful. Now I can see for myself how Jesus worms out of this one. It's one thing to allow gossip about miracles and healings, but now he must prove it to be true. The whole crowd will see him squirm. Smile, Jesus; you're about to be humiliated.

He's saying something to the fool on the mat. I'd better listen.

"Son, your sins are forgiven."

What! His sins are forgiven? No one can forgive sins except God alone. Jesus is a heretic, a blasphemer! Wait. Jesus is looking at me. I think he's going to say something to me. It had better be an apology, that's for sure. He can't heal, and he certainly has no authority to forgive sin. I listen as he speaks.

"Why are you thinking these things? Which is easier: to say to the paralytic, 'Your sins are forgiven,' or to say, 'Get up, take your mat and walk'? But that you may know that I have authority on earth to forgive sins, I tell you, young man, get up, take your mat, and go home."

Jesus is a fool! No—worse than that. He's deranged. This man on the mat has been paralyzed since birth. He can't walk.

But . . . but . . . I don't believe it! He walks! He is taking up his mat. He's leaving. Jesus . . . Jesus healed him. Jesus healed him.

Can this be the son of God? Does he have the authority of God to forgive sin? Can he . . . can he forgive my sin? Can Jesus forgive me?

GAME INSTRUCTIONS

Materials Needed: One photocopy of the game per player, pencils.

Approximate Playing Time: 2-3 minutes.

Special Instructions: Allow students to work in pairs.

After the Game: Review the various obstacles the paralyzed man and his friends had to bypass. Discussion Starters will help your students connect the story to their own personal needs.

TEACHING IDEAS

Materials Needed:

Object lesson: trash can, bits of trash, milk shake or ice-cold soda.

Learning project: comics, paste, pens or pencils, heavy paper, scissors, sample homemade comic strip.

Conclusion activity: index cards, pens.

Discussion Starters: Why did the men want to reach Jesus? Why do you think they were willing to stop at nothing to get to him? What were some of the obstacles they had to overcome? Today, what might be some things that could prevent people from finding Jesus? What two things did Jesus do for the man? Which do you think Jesus felt was most important? Why? What is sin and why does it need to be forgiven? Does God still forgive sin today? What are some things we do to become forgiven?

Object Lesson: Here's one that's been around some time, but it always works great. Before class, put crumpled paper and other bits of trash in a trash can. Purchase a milk shake or other refreshing drink.

When ready to do the object lesson, show the milk shake to your class. Ask for a show of hands from those who would like to have the shake to drink. Pick one student to come forward.

Say something like, *All right, you lucky person. Here's your shake. But first, let me do one thing.* Make a melodramatic show of dumping the trash out of the trash can. Pour the drink into the trash can. Hand it to the person to drink from. The learner will, of course, have an adverse reaction. Have the hapless volunteer sit down.

Explain, *There was nothing wrong with the drink. It was clean and good. It was, that is, until I poured it into the dirty trash can. There is a moral to my demonstration. Sin is like that dirt. It ruins the good things in a person. Sin makes us polluted in God's eyes. That is why we need to have our sin removed. God removes our sin by forgiving us.*

Learning Project: Buy some comic books or provide newspaper comic sections. Paste, pens or pencils, heavy paper, and scissors are also needed. It's a good idea to prepare a comic strip as described below to serve as an example to your students.

Tell students, *I want you to work together in groups of four or five to make a comic strip. Your comic strip should have several panels made from cartoon characters you are to cut out of the comics I'm giving you. The story should be about forgiveness. It can be a story about two friends who forgive each other for a fight they had, a story about the paralyzed man, or anything you can think of—as long as it has something to do with forgiveness. If you happen to have a super hero comic, maybe you could invent a super hero who brings the bad guys to Jesus.*

Let your kids use their imaginations. Their efforts may be uneven or off the mark, but you can use the opportunity, as you discuss each group's comic, to further explain the problem of sin and the need for God's loving forgiveness.

Conclusion Activity: Read 1 John 1:9 to your class, "If we confess our sins, he is faithful and just and will forgive us our sins and purify us from all unrighteousness." Be sure students understand all the terms used in the verse. To conclude the lesson, you can work with your class to memorize the verse, or students can paraphrase it in their own words and write it on a card to save or display at home.

Young people sometimes mistakenly believe that God must be begged for forgiveness, that he only forgives us because he has to. Be sure your learners understand that God loves to forgive us and strongly desires to hear our prayers.

THE A-Mazed Paralytic!

"Which is easier: to say to the paralytic, 'Your sins are forgiven,' or to say, 'Get up, take your mat and walk'? But that you may know that the Son of Man has authority on earth to forgive sins. . . ." He said to the paralytic, "I tell you, get up, take your mat and go home." He got up, took his mat and walked out in full view of them all (Mark 2:9-12).

Jesus is the source of healing, forgiveness, love, and salvation. If you correctly work this maze, you can help the paralyzed man and his friends get past all the obstacles to Jesus.

14. Jesus and the Demon-Possessed Man

Bible Passage: Luke 8:26-39.
Lesson Theme: Jesus is wise to
Satan's tricks.

STORY

Story Starter: Show your learners a pair of glasses, binoculars, or a telescope. Explain, *Glasses help a person see better. They bring things into sharp focus. Binoculars and telescopes allow us to learn about objects at great distances. All these things improve our vision. In the story I'm about to read, there is a startling example of Jesus' power to see things beyond a normal person's ability. I don't mean that he could see better with his eyes. Rather, Jesus demonstrated insight and understanding far beyond the commonplace.*

Mrs. Oliver walked into the little butcher shop. "Good day," she called to the butcher, Mr. Solomon.

"Good day to you, Mrs. Oliver," said Mr. Solomon with a smile. Mrs. Oliver had been a customer for many years. Mr. Solomon enjoyed her patronage, though she tended to haggle over prices. Mrs. Oliver examined the displays of meat, making disapproving noises over the posted dollar amounts.

"Mr. Solomon," she said with just the right touch of displeasure in her voice. "Mr. Solomon, how is an old woman like me supposed to stay alive when you charge such ridiculous sums of money for this meat?"

"My dear woman," replied Mr. Solomon, "my meats are very reasonably priced. They are the finest in the entire world. But it so happens that I have a very special deal for you today. Fresh, mouth-watering pork. Here it is, feast your eyes." With a flourish, Mr. Solomon unveiled a large pan heaped with raw pork chops.

"It looks fresh enough," sniffed Mrs. Oliver. "How much do you want for it, you old robber baron?"

Mr. Solomon named a very low price. So low, in fact, that Mrs. Oliver couldn't believe her ears.

"What's wrong with this meat?" she demanded.

"Why, nothing. I assure you, it is of the very highest standards." As he said this, Mr. Solomon crossed his fingers behind his back.

"I won't buy this meat unless you tell me why it's so cheap. Come clean, Mr. Solomon. What's the story behind this meat?"

Mr. Solomon came clean. This is what he told Mrs. Oliver.

The day before, Jesus had come to the region where Mrs. Oliver and Mr. Solomon lived. Just as he arrived, Jesus was met by a demon-possessed man from the town. For a long time, this man had not worn clothes or lived in a house, but had lived in the graveyard outside of town. When he saw Jesus, he cried out and fell at the Lord's feet, shouting at the top of his lungs, "What do you want with me, Jesus, Son of the Most High God? I beg you, don't torture me!"

The People Who
Brought You This Book...

—— *Invite you to discover MORE valuable youth ministry resources.* ——

uth Specialties offers an assortment of books, publications, tapes and events, all
signed to encourage and train youth workers and their kids. Just check what you're
terested in below and return this card, and we'll send you FREE information on our
oducts and services.

ease send me FREE information I've checked below:

The Complete Youth Specialties Catalog and information on upcoming Youth
Specialties events.

ume _____

dress _____

ty _____ State _____ Zip _____

one Number ( )_____

The People Who
Brought You This Book...

—— *Invite you to discover MORE valuable youth ministry resources.* ——

uth Specialties offers an assortment of books, publications, tapes and events, all
signed to encourage and train youth workers and their kids. Just check what you're
erested in below and return this card, and we'll send you FREE information on our
oducts and services.

ase send me FREE information I've checked below:

The Complete Youth Specialties Catalog and information on upcoming Youth
Specialties events.

me _____

dress _____

y _____ State _____ Zip _____

one Number ( )_____

Call for fast service:
(619) 440-2333

BUSINESS REPLY MAIL
FIRST CLASS   PERMIT NO. 16   EL CAJON, CA

POSTAGE WILL BE PAID BY ADDRESSEE

YOUTH SPECIALTIES
1224 Greenfield Dr.
El Cajon, CA 92021-9989

Call for fast service:
(619) 440-2333

NO POSTAG
NECESSAR
IF MAILED
IN THE
UNITED STAT

BUSINESS REPLY MAIL
FIRST CLASS   PERMIT NO. 16   EL CAJON, CA

POSTAGE WILL BE PAID BY ADDRESSEE

YOUTH SPECIALTIES
1224 Greenfield Dr.
El Cajon, CA 92021-9989

He said this because Jesus had recognized that the man was demon possessed. Many times the demon had seized him, and though he had been chained hand and foot and kept under guard, he had broken his chains and had been driven by the demon into solitary places.

Jesus asked him, "What is your name?"

"Legion," he replied, because many demons had gone into him. And they begged Jesus repeatedly not to order them to go back to hell.

At this point, Mrs. Oliver interrupted Mr. Solomon's discourse. "This man was demon possessed, you say? You mean controlled by the spirits of dead people?"

"No," replied Mr. Solomon. "Demons are not departed humans. Demons are bad angels. Angels that rebelled with Satan when he rebelled against God. God threw them out of heaven, long before humanity was created. Now some of them try to take control of human beings."

Mr. Solomon returned to his story.

A large herd of pigs was feeding there on the hillside. The demons begged Jesus to let them go into them, and he gave them permission. When the demons came out of the man, they went into the pigs, and the herd rushed down the steep bank into the lake and was drowned.

When the fellows tending the pigs saw what had happened, they ran off and reported this in the town and countryside, and the people went out to see what had happened. When they came to Jesus, they found the man from whom the demons had gone out, sitting at Jesus' feet, dressed, and in his right mind; and they were afraid.

Those who had seen it told the people how the demon-possessed man had been cured. Then all the people of the region asked Jesus to leave them, because they were overcome with fear. So he left.

The man whom Jesus saved wanted to follow the Lord, but Jesus told him to go back and spread the news to the entire town.

"Return home and tell how much God has done for you," Jesus instructed him. So the man went away and told the whole town how much Jesus had done for him.

Mrs. Oliver looked sternly at Mr. Solomon. After a lengthy pause, during which Mr. Solomon gulped and shifted his feet nervously, Mrs. Oliver spoke. "Do you mean to tell me that this is demon-possessed pork from drowned pigs?" She spoke in a low voice.

"I didn't mean to tell you, Madam. You wheedled it out of me. I suppose now you won't want to buy it. Nobody wants to buy it. All my customers have run out of the store when they heard where it came from."

"Nonsense," exclaimed Mrs. Oliver. "I will buy it. The price is very reasonable. I never pass up a good bargain."

Mr. Solomon was shocked. "B-But Mrs. Oliver," he stammered. "Aren't you afraid that this meat is demon possessed?"

"No, why should I be? For meat this cheap, I'll just go find Jesus, and he can cast out any evil spirits in it."

❖ ❖ ❖

After the Story: Your students will be naturally curious about demon possession. Some children may even worry about it. Take a few minutes to explain that Christians need not fear being possessed by evil spirits, for we are possessed by God. Jesus, as demonstrated in the story, has complete authority over the powers of evil. The "Jesus Versus the Devil" game helps drive this idea home.

GAME INSTRUCTIONS

Materials Needed: One photocopy of the game for each pair of players, pencils.

Approximate Playing Time: 3-5 minutes.

Special Instructions: Hand out games—one game for each pair of players. Read the verse and instructions as students follow along. Demonstrate the sample game. The puzzle solution is at the back of the book.

TEACHING IDEAS

Materials Needed:

Learning project: pencil and paper for each learner.

Discussion Starters: Why were the demons and the people afraid of Jesus? How do you think Jesus was able to know this man was possessed rather than just crazy? Does Jesus know things we don't know, such as the future? What are some ways that Jesus' ability to know things can be used to help us in our own lives?

Learning Project: Give each person a pencil and paper. Say, ***Number your papers one through ten. I am now going to read ten statements. The statements are either true or false. Write a T for true and an F for false. Does everyone understand?***

There is one small string attached to this assignment. I want you to list your ten answers before I read the statements. That's right. List your answers now, and then I will read the statements. We'll see how well you can do.

Allow students to list their answers, then read the statements aloud.
1. The teacher's nose looks like a yellow banana.
2. I'm a girl.
3. My name is Phineas J. Dorklemeyer.
4. The person sitting next to me is the biggest hunk in the world.
5. The teacher drools a lot.
6. I'm three years old.
7. I'm married and have thirteen kids.
8. My favorite food is snail meat.
9. I'm wearing boys' clothes.
10. I'm an alien from the planet Borx.

Have fun with your class, then say something like, ***It's nearly impossible to get all ten answers correct just by chance. But if we somehow had the ability to know the statements before they were read, we could get them all right.***

It's the same in our lives. We don't know what tomorrow brings. But Jesus does. With the same supernatural insight and power he used to detect and defeat Satan, Jesus knows things we can't know, and he knows what to do. It makes sense for us to let him guide us through our lives.

Conclusion Activity: Play some guessing games (your weight and age, number of beans in a jar, how many seconds a student can hold his or her breath, and so on). Point out, ***Life can sometimes be a bit of a guessing game. We may not know what to do. But God always knows. Let's ask him to be our guide in life.***

Jesus versus the Devil

When they came to Jesus, they found the man from whom the demons had gone out, sitting at Jesus' feet, dressed and in his right mind; and they were afraid (Luke 8:35).

The evil spirits were terrified of the Lord Jesus. The people who saw him cast out the demons were also frightened. Even the people who just heard about it were quaking in their sandals. Why? Because Jesus had something they had never seen before. To find out what, grab a friend and solve this puzzle.

Sample game:

$$C + \text{(hat)} - H = Cat$$

(C + HAT – H = CAT)

(See Solution Sheet for the answer.)

15. Jesus Feeds 5,000

> **Bible Passage:** John 6:1-15.
> **Lesson Theme:** Jesus is the Bread of Life.

STORY

Story Starter: Your students might enjoy beginning the lesson with a game of "Hangman." They are to guess the word *bread*. Draw five blanks on a poster or chalkboard, representing the five letters in bread. Also draw a noose.

Have somebody guess a letter. If the letter is in *bread*, write it on the proper blank. If the letter is incorrect, draw a circle representing a head on the noose. Add a body part (body, arm, leg, hand, foot) each time an incorrect guess is made. Give everyone a chance to guess a letter. The first student to recognize the word wins. No one wins if the hanged man is completed. Say, ***Bread is correct. Today we are going to take a look at Jesus, who called himself the Bread of Life.***

❖ ❖ ❖

"Good morning, sports fans! Welcome to *The World of Sports*. This is Kim Loudmouth, and with me here in the booth is Tim Blowhard, former coach of the Jerusalem Tigers. Well, Tim, it looks like a beautiful day for a game."

"It sure does, Kim. The forecast is for great weather all morning, though a quick storm might blow in off the lake later tonight. But right now it's sunny and warm with very little wind. A perfect day to see some real action on the field. I'm excited."

"That's right, Tim. Well, folks, we certainly will see some great action today. Five thousand fans have packed the stadium here overlooking the Sea of Galilee. Right now, let's go down to the field to our own Jim Waterboy with one of his famous up-close-and-personal looks at some of the sports legends that are here to play. Jim?"

"Thanks, Kim. Er, there seems to be a bit of a problem down here on the field, Kim."

"And what might that problem be, Jim?"

"Uh . . . well, I can't seem to find any players, Kim."

"No players, Jim?"

"No, Kim. As a matter of fact, I can't even find a stadium."

"Excuse me, Jim Waterboy. This is coach Tim Blowhard up in the booth. Did you say there are no players and no stadium?"

"That's right, Tim. All I see are 5,000 people sitting on the grass. I can see your booth, too. But that's all."

"You know, Jim Waterboy, now that you mention it, I don't see any stadium either. No teams, no stadium. Just 5,000 people sitting on the grass. Kim Loudmouth, do you have any ideas?"

"We'll be right back after these important messages.

"Okay, we're off the air. Listen, Waterboy, what do you mean there's no players? Do you hear me, Waterboy?"

"Yes, Kim. Look, I'm sorry, but we've got the wrong place. There's no game here. This is just a mountain meadow that just happens to have 5,000 fans."

"Just happens to have 5,000 fans, huh? Listen, Waterboy. You take that microphone of yours, and you find somebody who can tell us what's happening here. And find out fast. We'll be back from commercial in 30 seconds."

"We're back live at . . . at . . . uh, we're back live, folks. Now let's go back down to the field to our own Jim Waterboy. Jim?"

"Thanks, Kim. With me now is a fine athlete named, uh . . . "

"Andrew, sir."

"Andrew. Are you the Andrew who played for the Jericho Jets?"

"No, sir. I'm just plain Andrew, Simon Peter's brother."

"Simon Peter. The fleet-footed running back from Temple University."

"No. Simon Peter the humble fisherman from the Sea of Galilee."

"Oh, yeah. Well, I'm sure you and your brother have come ready to play. Tell me, what's your game plan for today? Are you going to run on most downs or are you going to rely on the pass?"

"Frankly, sir, I have no idea what you are talking about. Everybody's here to listen to the Lord Jesus Christ. Five thousand people have come to hear his wisdom."

"Every team needs a wise coach, son. Er, just what position do you play?"

"Jesus sent me to find something for the crowd to eat. He said, 'Where shall we buy bread for these people to eat?' So I went looking for someone with food."

"Oh. Well, I think the concession stands might be over that way."

"I already found the food. I came across a little boy with a lunch bag. He had five small barley loaves and two small fish. I took him to Jesus."

"Excuse me, Jim Waterboy. This is Kim Loudmouth in the booth. We'll get back to the sports action after this word from our sponsor."

"We're back. Jim Waterboy is down on the field. Jim?"

"Right, Kim. I've had a chance to locate the great coach of Andrew's team. His name is Jesus Christ, and right now he's talking to his 12-man team (known as the Disciples, by the way) and to the crowd of 5,000 cheering fans. Let's listen in if we can."

"Have the people sit down."

"Excuse me, Jim Waterboy. This is Tim Blowhard up in the booth. It's hard to hear Coach Jesus over the crowd noise. What did he say?"

"He told the people to sit down. They're sitting down now, and I think things will grow quiet so he can be clearly heard."

"Just what is he doing now, Jim?"

"Very strange, Tim. It looks like he's taking some food. Yes, it's the bread and fish Andrew found. Jesus is giving thanks for the food and breaking it into bits."

"Giving thanks? To the little boy who brought the food?"

"No. Giving thanks to God in heaven. He's praying. Now he and the disciples are handing out the food. Wait a minute. This is amazing. Jesus is handing out food to dozens of people. No, make that hundreds. It's miraculous! Somehow Jesus has multiplied the fish and loaves into enough food to feed all 5,000 people. Everybody is eating. Everybody is full.

"Now the disciples are sweeping up the leftovers. There's 12 big baskets full of leftovers. The crowd is screaming and cheering!"

"Uh, thanks, Jim Waterboy. This is one play that will definitely make the sports highlights on the evening news. That wraps up this edition of *The World of Sports*. Our final score: Jesus, 5,000. For Tim Blowhard and Jim Waterboy, this is Kim Loudmouth saying so long."

❖ ❖ ❖

GAME INSTRUCTIONS

Materials Needed: One photocopy of the game for each group of two or three players, scissors, corrugated cardboard, thumbtacks.

Approximate Playing Time: 6-8 minutes.

Special Instructions: This isn't a game as much as it is an astonishing puzzler. Distribute a game copy, scissors, thumbtack, and piece of cardboard to each group of two or three students. The students cut the game apart and tack the pieces together using the cardboard as a backing for the tack. Read the instructions aloud.

After the Game: Challenge players to explain how the game works. (We don't know either!) Say, *Jesus didn't use a trick like this one to feed the crowd. He did it by the miraculous power of God. The day after Jesus fed the crowd, people came to him asking for more food. He told them that what they really needed was the Bread of Life. What is the Bread of Life? Let's find out.*

TEACHING IDEAS

Materials Needed:

Learning project: colored markers, a small or medium box, several verses written one per index card.

Conclusion activity: doughnuts for all learners.

Learning Project:

Provide each group of three to five students with colored markers and a box. Any sort of box will do, such as a cereal box, shoe box, or fruit crate. However, the box must be plain so that students can write and draw on it. If necessary, cover it with paper.

Hand out copies of the following verses to each group:

"Do not work for food that spoils, but for food that endures to eternal life" (John 6:27).

"For the bread of God is he who comes down from heaven and gives life to the world" (John 6:33).

"I am the bread of life. He who comes to me will never go hungry, and he who believes in me will never be thirsty" (John 6:35).

"If a man eats of this bread, he will live forever" (John 6:51).

Explain, *When the people came to Jesus looking for a free meal, he told them that they should seek the Bread of Life. He went on to explain that he is the Bread of Life. What did he mean? He meant that if a person wants to live forever in heaven, he or she must come to Jesus, who is the source of spiritual life, just as regular food is the source of regular life. The Bible verses I've given you help explain this.*

Tell your students that each group is going to design a box that contains Bread of Life, like a cereal box contains cereal. They are to design the package art and list all the good things about the Bread (as found in the verses).

Let them have fun with this project, then permit a time of displaying and discussing the results.

Conclusion Activity:

If you want to surprise your class with a special treat, hand out doughnuts. Say, *Since we have been talking about the Bread of Life, I thought you might enjoy a little snack.*

Work together with your students to memorize John 6:35.

MULTIPLYING FISH

"Here is a boy with five small barley loaves and two small fish, but how far will they go among so many?" (John 6:9).

Pretty far! After Jesus gave thanks for the loaves and fish, he broke them into pieces and let his disciples hand them out to thousands of people. Afterward, they filled 12 baskets with the leftovers. Another example of the Lord's amazing power.

Well, here's a strange puzzler that will help you turn 12 fish into 13. It's incredible—try it. Carefully cut out the shaded circle. Push a tack through the center dot into the center dot of the other circle. To make an extra fish appear, move the center arrow from point A to point B. Weird, eh?

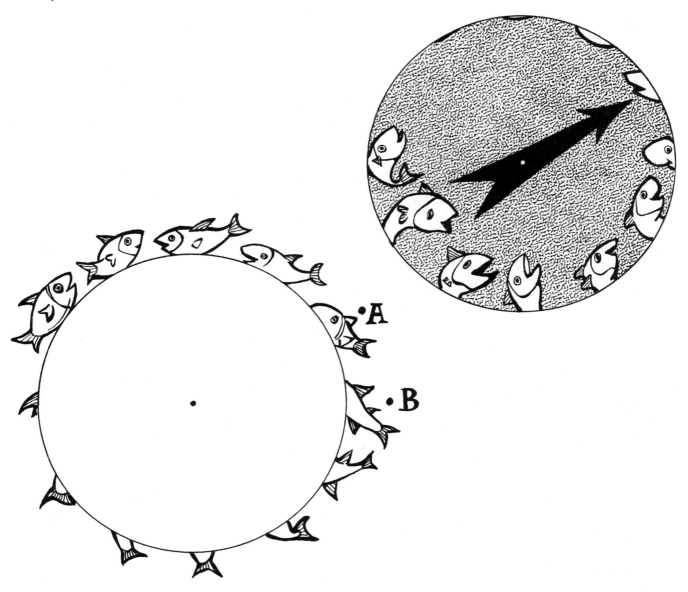

When you play or think about this puzzler, remember the Lord's miracle of the fish and the bread. Show the game to your friends and family.

16. The Transfiguration

Bible Passage: Exodus 33:18-23; Luke 9:28-36.
Lesson Theme: Jesus is God's son.

STORY

Story Starter: Show your students a rock and a light bulb. Point to a door. Say, *I want you to think about Jesus Christ as I ask you a question. What do this rock, that door, and the light from this bulb have in common?* Allow students to hazard a few guesses. The three things represent three names that Jesus was called: the rock (1 Corinthians 10:4), the door (John 10:9), and the light (John 8:12).

Explain, *Jesus had many names and titles that help us to understand what he is like. We'll play a game that features many more of these names and titles. Right now, as I read the story, see if you can pick up the one title mentioned that tells us something very important about who Jesus is.*

Our story is about Jesus, but it begins many centuries before he came to earth as a baby, born in Bethlehem. It begins in a little tent in the desert, where Moses is talking to the Lord God. Moses has been obediently doing all the things God has asked, so the Lord is pleased. In the glow of the moment, Moses asks a favor.

"Lord, show me your glory."

Now, up to that time no one had seen God in his full glory, for God's appearance is so awesome and majestic that a person who saw him would drop dead on the spot. So the thing Moses asked was not quite appropriate.

God said, "I will cause all my goodness to pass in front of you. But you cannot see my face, for no one may see me and live. There is a place near me where you may stand on a rock. When my glory passes by, I will put you in a cleft in the rock and cover you with my hand until I have passed by. Then I will remove my hand and you will see my back; but my face must not be seen."

And so it happened that Moses got to see God's glory, but not his face. His prayer request was granted, but not fully.

Now let's leap forward in time to the days when Jesus lived on earth. By then Moses had been dead for centuries. Let's look in on Jesus and his disciples as something unexpected happens to Moses. As we'll see, his prayer is about to be answered here on earth—not too many miles from where Moses talked to God in that little tent.

Let's imagine that we are looking at a page from a diary that Peter, the big fisherman who had become one of Jesus' closest disciples, might have written. Peter tells about the day he and his friends saw the glory of God in the face of Jesus.

Dear Diary:

You won't believe what happened today. Never in the history of the world has anyone seen God's face and lived. But today I saw the glory of God—and I'm still breathing.

Jesus took three of us—James, John, and me—up to a mountain to pray. It was a long walk and James, John, and I were exhausted. But we woke up fast when we saw what happened next.

Jesus had gone off a little way to pray. As he was praying, the appearance of his face changed, and his clothes became as bright as lightning bolts. Two men, Moses and Elijah the prophet, appeared in heavenly splendor, talking with Jesus. I don't know how I knew it was them, since they had died centuries before I was born, but somehow I knew. They spoke with Jesus for some time.

I was so astonished by this appearance of God's glory on Jesus' face that I blurted, "Let's build three shelters—one for Jesus, one for Moses, and one for Elijah." I don't know why I said such a stupid thing. I guess I was trying to keep Moses, Elijah, and Jesus together forever so people could view them like fish in an aquarium. My brain just went numb when I saw God's face. Jesus had taken on his true heavenly appearance.

A strange cloud suddenly appeared and enveloped everyone. John, James, and I were terrified as we entered the cloud. God's voice came from the cloud, saying, "This is my Son, whom I have chosen; listen to him." Then the voice, the cloud, and Moses and Elijah disappeared. Jesus' radiant appearance returned to normal.

I don't know about you, Diary, but I don't think I'm going to tell anyone about this for a while. At least until I stop shaking.

Good-bye for now.

The Bible tells us that Peter, James, and John didn't tell anyone about the glory of God on Christ's face for a long time.

❖ ❖ ❖

After the Story: Be sure your students comprehend how Moses' original prayer was, in a sense, answered at Christ's Transfiguration. Remind them that the story contained one of Jesus' titles. Did anyone catch it? It was "Son," spoken by God from the cloud.

GAME INSTRUCTIONS

Materials Needed: One photocopy of the game for each group of two or three players, pencils.

Approximate Playing Time: 8-10 minutes.

Special Instructions: Hand out copies of the game, one per team of two or three students. The team works together to find all the words. Teams can play against each other in a more competitive version of this game if you allow only a short time in which to find as many words as possible. When time is up, award one point for *each letter* in each word correctly circled. That way, the kids who found the longer words will likely win. Subtract points for incorrect words.

After the Game: As time permits, discuss the meaning and significance of each name and title. See the solution sheet to find all the names.

Materials Needed:

Learning project: notebook paper and pencils.

Conclusion activity: drawing paper, colored pens.

Other Bible Passages: Here are a few of the many verses that express the idea that Christians are children of God: Romans 8:14-17; Galatians 3:26-4:71; 1 John 3:1.

Discussion Starters: What was Moses' request? How was it answered? When God spoke to Jesus' disciples, who did he say Jesus was? Why do you suppose it was important for the disciples to know this? What did God tell the disciples to do? How can we listen to Jesus today?

Learning Project: The point of this project is to show that, although fully God, Jesus became human like us. He understands us and has gone through all the things we face in life. God knows how we feel and is near to us.

Ask your students to think about cats. Say, *I want you to work together in small groups to make a list of things cats do that make them . . . well, cats. For example, how do cats clean themselves? With their tongues. Write that down. And what do cats eat? Put that on your list. Come up with at least five things that make a cat a cat.*

When done, discuss what they have noted.

Now ask, *How do we human beings do the things on your list? For example, how do we clean ourselves? What do we eat? Could we imitate the way cats do these things? Do you think we could imitate them so well that a real cat would be fooled into thinking we are cats? In order for us to truly experience the life of a cat, we would have to become cats. God came to earth to experience being human. Jesus was and is fully God. He took on human flesh so that he could feel what we feel and experience what we experience. He fully understands us because he became one of us. He is God's son, fully God and completely human.*

Conclusion Activity: Read John 1:12 to your students, "Yet to all who received him, to those who believed in his name, he gave the right to become children of God." Explain, *This verse tells us that if we believe in Jesus and receive him as our Lord and Savior, God will adopt us into his heavenly family to be his children. We won't be God like Jesus is, but we will be sons and daughters of God.*

I want you to grab a sheet of paper. At the top write, "I will take these two important steps." Draw two large footprints on your paper. In one footprint write, Believe. In the other write, Receive. Then sign your name. Hang the paper on your bedroom wall as a reminder.

THE Son of God

A voice came from the cloud, saying, "This is my Son, whom I have chosen; listen to him" (Luke 9:35).

In the verse above, Jesus is called "God's Son." The Bible also has a lot of other names and titles for him. When we take a look at them, we learn more about Jesus' nature. For example, the Bible calls him "King." That tells us that he is in charge. We've put 17 of Jesus' names and titles in this word game. See how many you can find and circle. The words run vertically, horizontally, and diagonally, and they may share letters.

17. The Rich Young Man

Bible Passage: Mark 10:17-27.
Lesson Theme: Don't let anything stand
between you and God.

STORY

Story Starter: Tell your learners, ***The first part of my story is from the Bible. It is recorded in Mark 10:17-27.***

One day as Jesus was traveling along, a young man ran up to him. The man fell on his knees before the Lord and asked, "What must I do to gain eternal life in heaven?"

Jesus asked the man if he had kept the commandments that God had carved on stone tablets and given to Moses.

"Teacher," the young man declared, "I have kept them all since I was a boy."

Jesus felt love for the young man, knowing that he had done his best to honor God by obeying the commandments. But Jesus also knew that the young man had a problem. He loved money more than God.

"If you want to get to heaven, you must sell everything you have and give the money to the poor so that you can follow me. If you do this, you will have riches in heaven."

At this the man's face fell. He went away sad, because he had great wealth.

The Bible doesn't tell us what happened next to the rich young man, but perhaps it went something like the following:

"Sell everything I have and give the money to the poor? If he thinks I'm going to give up all my riches so I can follow him and his dusty band of disciples, he'll just have to do without me. Hey, I've kept the commandments. Well, sort of. Nobody's perfect, you know."

As he mumbled and grumbled his way down the path, the young man came to an office building. He walked across the lobby and looked at the directory. He found the office he was looking for: Phineas Snodgrass, Income Tax Collector.

The young man went into the office. A secretary ushered him into a rear office to meet Phineas Snodgrass himself. The little man sat behind a big desk stacked with papers.

"I see by your file that you have problems, young man." The expression on the tax collector's face reflected a certain anticipation, like a wolf about to carve up a lamb.

"Probems, sir?" gulped the young man. "Well, you see, it's like this—"

"I'll tell you what it's like," said the tax collector grimly. "You haven't paid your taxes in five years. You are going to jail. We are taking everything you own!"

And that's just what happened.

After the Story: Explain that we do not know what happened to the rich young man just after he rejected Jesus. But we do know what happened to him in the long run. He died. And no matter how much money he had, he lost it all. Ask your students, ***Do you think the man made a good decision?***

GAME INSTRUCTIONS

Materials Needed: One photocopy of the game per player, one enlarged copy of the game, coins, pencils, masking tape.

Approximate Playing Time: 5-10 minutes.

Special Instructions: If your photocopier enlarges, enlarge the game onto an 11" x 17" page. Provide a coin and a pencil for each player, and mark a foul line on the floor with tape. Alternate rules: If you haven't enough room to toss coins, set the game pages on tables. Players use one coin to bat another coin toward the target, as shown in the illustration.

After the Game: Let students tally their scores. Collect the coins. Involve students in thinking about the point of the story and game by using Discussion Starters.

TEACHING IDEAS

Materials Needed:

Learning project: several verses written on notebook paper, one verse per page.

Conclusion activity: construction paper or index cards, pens.

Discussion Starters: What was the one thing that kept the young man in our story from giving his life completely to God? What was it Jesus told the man to give up so that he could follow him? What are some of the things the person in the game was carrying? Most of these things aren't bad. In fact, they are good unless they stand between a person and God. Let's talk about how these things might come between a person and the Lord.

Object Lesson: Your students can be involved in this object lesson. Point to the room's door and say something like, *The door can be closed and locked to keep things out of the room. It blocks the wind, it keeps people out, and it stops bugs and animals from intruding into our room. Can you tell me what the window screens block out? What about the glass in the windows?*

You can name other things in the room designed to block things out, such as the walls, the roof, and the heater (which blocks the discomfort of chilly air). Explain that the purpose of all these objects is to block things out. But the rich young man's great wealth blocked God out of his life. Nothing is supposed to separate us from our Lord.

Learning Project: Give each group of two or three students a copy of one of the verses below, a different verse for each group. Say, *I want you to scramble the words in your Bible verse so that each word is unrecognizable. Don't scramble the book in which the verse is found and don't change the order of the words in the verse. Then I'll have you switch verses with another group, and you can solve someone else's scrambled verse.* If a group finds it impossible to solve a word, reveal it to them or allow them to use a Bible.

When all the verses have been unscrambled, ask a member of each group to read the verse. Tell your learners, *We've been talking about things that can block us or separate us from God. Each verse that you've unscrambled mentions one thing that is the opposite of a block—a thing that tends to draw us closer to God. I want each group to figure out what that thing is, then be ready to tell us all.*

Let the word of Christ dwell in you richly (Colossians 3:16).

"Trust in God; trust also in me" (John 14:1).

"You are my friends if you do what I command" (John 15:14).

Devote yourselves to prayer (Colossians 4:2).

All the believers were together (Acts 2:44).

You are looking for the following things, in the order of the above verses: reading the Bible, faith in God, obedience to God, prayer, and fellowship with Christian friends.

Discuss how these things draw a person closer to God.

Conclusion Activity: Read Revelation 3:20: "Here I am! I stand at the door and knock. If anyone hears my voice and opens the door, I will come in and eat with him, and he with me." Explain that the verse is a promise made by Jesus, who will come into a person's life if that person will only clear the path by removing things that stand in the way. Give each student a few minutes to construct a paper door labeled, "Jesus said, 'If anyone opens the door, I will come in,' (Revelation 3:20)." The door can be kept in a purse, wallet, Bible, or posted in a bedroom.

BOWLING FOR BURDENS

Jesus looked at him and loved him. "One thing you lack," he said. "Go, sell everything you have and give to the poor, and you will have treasure in heaven. Then come, follow me."
At this the man's face fell. He went away sad, because he had great wealth (Mark 10:21, 22).

Too much junk. The rich man missed heaven because he didn't want to let go of the stuff he had on earth.

On this page is a picture of a guy carrying a lot of junk. You can help him get rid of it. If you help him drop everything, he can follow Jesus and you win the game!

Place this sheet of paper on the floor against a wall, and toss a coin at it. If the coin touches one or more pieces of junk, check off the junk with a pencil, and give yourself ten points for each piece. If your coin misses, subtract two points. Don't double count a piece of junk that's been checked off. Take turns with a friend or two and keep score.

18. Blind Bartimaeus

Bible Passage: Mark 10:46-52.
Lesson Theme: Spiritual sight.

STORY

Story Starter: Blindfold one or two students and ask them to perform this task: While their classmates shout directions, the students attempt to locate a few candy bars or other prizes that you've placed on the floor.

When the blindfolds have been removed, tell your learners, *Today I want to tell you a story about a man named Bartimaeus. Like a person wearing a blindfold, he couldn't see. He was born blind. Happily, a wonderful thing happened to him.*

If you happen to have a blind student, you might invite him or her to share insights about being blind as you describe Bartimaeus.

Imagine that you are a sewer worker. It's your job to crawl down into the slimy, mucky storm drains to keep things flowing. You live and labor in a boring little country town named Jericho, plopped in the desert a few miles beyond Jerusalem.

It's lunch time in the drainpipe, so you sit on the bottom rung of your ladder, get out your bag, and dig into a tough, gristly sandwich.

As you sit in your pipe, kicking mud balls and gnashing at the sandwich, you think about how dull life is in Jericho. Oh, sure, you've heard the stories about how God made the walls fall down. But that was centuries ago. And besides, that was a different Jericho. Nope. Nothing happened yesterday, nothing has happened today, and nothing will happen tomorrow. At least it's not raining. Cleaning a drainpipe is murder during a rainstorm.

From overhead comes the sound of someone shouting. As you prick up your ears, you hear the faint noise of a distant crowd. Intrigued, you climb up the ladder, crack open the manhole cover, and take a peek up and down the town's wide, dusty main street.

Off to your right, sitting cross-legged on the curb, is a filthy, blind beggar. You are sure that if you didn't smell so bad yourself you would get a nose full of the grubby guy. He's parked at that very spot all day, every day, begging for the few crumbs and rags he receives. His name is Bartimaeus, but everyone calls him old Bart. Old Bart is the only guy in town with a job worse than yours—begging.

The noise that got your attention is getting louder. Doors and windows are coming open as the citizens of Jericho look to see what all the commotion is about. Why, it sounds like a riot is coming this way. You turn your head to look back up the street. It is a riot! There's a huge crowd of people pounding rapidly toward you and the center of town. Some of the people you recognize as fellow Jeri-coneheads, the rest are strangers.

"Look, it's Jesus," yells a woman from a second floor window. "It's Jesus!"

You've heard about him. People say he's the Son of God. They claim he heals people and raises the dead. Nonsense, you snort. Fairy tales for little kids.

The crowd has come much closer. People are cheering, some are waving pieces of brightly colored cloth. Everyone is trying to get a look at the man they've all heard about: Jesus, the son of God. The racket from the crowd is making your ears ring in the pipe's confined space. Suddenly, above all the din, come the agonized shouts of a man, "Jesus, Son of David, have mercy on me!"

It's blind Bart. Wow, you didn't know he had that kind of volume in his skinny body. Screaming in desperation and frustration, he keeps repeating the words, "Jesus, Son of David, have mercy on me!"

Many people in the crowd tell him to keep his mouth shut and stop causing trouble. Nobody wants Jesus to think Jericho is filled with old idiots, you know. Hey, if Jesus thinks Jericho is a nice, friendly, clean town, he and his hundreds of friends might stay over a few days, spending lots of money. Wouldn't that be fine? Unless Bart messes it up for us. "Shut up, Bart!"

Oh, no. Here comes Jesus. The crowd has parted, and you can see him clearly as you peek up from under the slightly raised lid.

"Call him," Jesus says, pointing to Bart. Jesus' voice is deep and strong. His expression shows great intelligence and wisdom, and the way he carries himself indicates an unusual strength of character. You gasp in surprise. Even from your hiding place you can almost touch the love and godliness that seems to radiate from the man. For a moment you believe the rumors of miracles—almost.

"Call him," Jesus says. Immediately people rush to Bart's side. "Cheer up! On your feet. He's calling you." Boy, has this crowd changed its tune. Throwing his tattered cloak aside, Bart jumps to his feet and comes to Jesus.

"What do you want me to do for you?" Jesus asks.

"Teacher, I want to see."

"Go," Jesus says. "Your faith has made you well."

Two things immediately happen. First, Bart blinks his eyes, turns around and yells, "I can see!" Second, as the crowd starts cheering in amazement, you slip off your ladder and land face down with a painful thump on the muddy floor of the pipe.

Crawling shakily up the ladder, stars whirling around your eyes, you once again peer out from under the manhole cover. Jesus and Bart are walking joyfully up the street, followed by the cheering, singing crowd. No one notices you. No one, that is, except Jesus, who gives you a wink as he passes by.

GAME INSTRUCTIONS

Materials Needed: One photocopy of the game per player, pencils.

Approximate Playing Time: 3-5 minutes.

Special Instructions: Hand out one game to each player. Read the game's Bible passage and instructions aloud. Gather players into pairs. One player in each pair closes his or her eyes and attempts to draw a line along the pipes from the sewer worker to the light above while the other player calls out directions. Allow players to switch.

After the Game: Tell the learners, *Jesus is the one who's calling out directions for our lives, and it is listening to Jesus' directions that takes us to life in the light instead of the darkness.* Be sure to connect the concept and difficulties of physical blindness with the concept and difficulties of spiritual blindness. Here is a list of ideas to get you started.

1. Physical blindness makes it difficult to know what is around you. It makes it hard to know which way to go. Spiritual blindness makes it hard to live your life wisely because you don't understand God's wisdom and guidance.

2. Physical blindness reduces your personal freedom; you often need help to do things you want to do. A spiritually blind person's only hope is to depend completely on Jesus.

3. Physical blindness reduces your ability to enjoy the beauty of God's creation. Spiritual insight allows a person to see God at work in the world and in his or her own life.

TEACHING IDEAS

Materials Needed:

Learning project: different colors of poster board, pens, masking tape.

Other Bible Passages: To help your students learn more about spiritual blindness—and spiritual sight—read John 9:39-41 and 1 Peter 1:5-9.

Discussion Starters: From the way the story made it sound, how often do you think Jesus passed through Jericho? What might have happened if Bartimaeus had decided to not ask for Jesus' help until the next time he came through town? What does this tell you about coming to God for help or love?

Bartimaeus believed in Jesus. Though he was physically blind, he had the "eyes" of faith to see that Jesus is the Son of God. A person who does not believe in Jesus can be called spiritually blind. Was the imaginary sewer worker spiritually blind? How can a spiritually blind person receive sight?

After he received his sight, Bartimaeus followed Jesus up the road. Why do you suppose he did so? How can a person follow Jesus today?

Learning Project: Give students an opportunity to use poster materials to make traffic signs with spiritual slogans. For example, "STOP what you're doing and YIELD to God!" The idea is that God should direct our lives just as road signs direct traffic.

Conclusion Activity: Let students post their signs in the halls and by doorways.

Stuck IN THE PIPES!

In him was life, and that life was the light of men. The light shines in the darkness, but the darkness has not understood it (John 1:4, 5).

Jesus is the light that lights up our lives. He not only can restore sight to blind people like Bartimaeus, but he can also give us the spiritual understanding and insight we need to live our lives as God wants us to.

Remember the silly sewer worker down in the drainpipes? He's still down there, as you can see if you take a look at the bottom of this page. He wants to come up through the manhole to the sunny day above. The trouble is, it's very dark in the pipes and he cannot see. Your job is to take your pencil and draw a line from the worker to the light. Sound too easy? It is, except for one thing: you have to close your eyes as you draw the line along the pipes. If the line you draw goes off the edge of a pipe, you lose!

It would be much easier to win this game if you kept your eyes open. Blindness makes it very hard to stay on the right path. In the same way, it is a lot easier to live a happy, satisfying life if you walk in the spiritual light with Jesus Christ. Let the Lord be your guide. Keep your eyes open and on Jesus.

19. The Parable of the Talents

Bible Passage: Matthew 25:14-30.
Lesson Theme: God-given talents.

STORY

Story Starter: Say to your learners, *You know what the word talent means, don't you? Sure. It's a special skill or ability, such as playing the piano or shooting baskets. I believe that there are many talents hidden inside each of us. These special gifts can be brought out with the proper encouragement. For example, you might have the talent to be a great actor, even though you've never been on the stage. With training and experience, you could become a famous star.*

It might surprise you to learn that the word talent *comes from the name of an ancient coin, called a "talent." Now, how do you suppose the name of a coin became the word for a special skill or ability? Give up? It's because of the Lord Jesus. Jesus told a story about some men who received some talents—the coin, that is. Let me tell you the Lord's story, and then perhaps you can tell me how our word* talent *came to be.*

A rich man was about to leave on a long vacation. He called his three servants to him to receive final instructions. He assigned each servant a portion of his wealth, and each servant was to take care of the money he was given. That way, the rich man's fortune would be safe until his return.

One slave was exceptionally bright, so the rich man entrusted five talents to him. In those days, a single talent was worth more than $1,000. If these men were earning the type of salary normally paid to a servant, it would have taken each of them more than 16 years just to earn one talent. Can you figure out how long it would take to earn five talents? The answer is more than 80 years!

The second servant was not as capable as the first one, so the rich man gave him two talents. Still, that was a lot of money, and the servant was probably proud of the trust his boss had in him. The final servant was given one talent.

The rich man went on his trip. I don't know where he went. If it was me, I'd go to Hawaii. But in those days, most people went to Rome or some other city. So he left, and the servants remained behind to take care of his fortune.

The first slave with the five talents put his money to work. I don't know what he did with the money, for Jesus didn't say. Somehow, whether through clever trading or buying and selling, the man was able to double his master's money. He ended up with ten talents. Truly a talented servant.

The second servant also doubled his money. He earned two more talents for a total of four. But the man with one talent went off and dug a hole in the ground. He threw the talent in and covered it up.

When the rich man returned, he called his servants in to give an account of what they had accomplished with the money. Servant number one said, "Master, you entrusted me with five talents. See, I have earned you five more."

His master replied, "Well done, good and faithful servant! You have been faithful with a few things; I will put you in charge of many things. Come and share your master's happiness!"

Servant number two said, "Master, you entrusted me with two talents. See, I have earned you two more. Pretty cool, eh?"

Again his master exclaimed, "Well done, good and faithful servant! You have been faithful with a few things; I will put you in charge of many things. Come and share your master's happiness!"

But then the third servant came. He said, "Master, I know that you are a hard man, ruthless with your money. I was afraid that I might lose the talent, so I hid it in a ditch. I dug it up. Here is what belongs to you."

The rich man was very angry with the servant. He called him lazy and wicked. He said, "You should have deposited the money in a bank so that I could at least have earned interest." The rich man grabbed the talent and gave it to the servant with ten talents. Then he had the miserable servant thrown off his property into the darkness.

After the Story: Say, *Now I want you to think about the Lord's story.* Then ask, *Can you tell me how our word talent, which means special skill or ability, came from this tale? What do you think Jesus was trying to teach us?*

GAME INSTRUCTIONS

Materials Needed: One photocopy of the game per player, pencils, scissors, paper.

Approximate Playing Time: 5-10 minutes, depending on the number of rounds played.

Special Instructions: Play this game yourself before playing it with students, just to be sure you understand it. Assemble players into groups of two or three. Hand out the game—one copy per player. As you read aloud, have players do the following:

1. Cut out the five cards. Pick one card that features the talent you think you might have (acing, drawing, music, being smart, or no talent). Set that one card off to the side. Shuffle the four remaining cards and place them face up in two pairs in front of you.

2. Look at the first pair. Does the color of the hair match (black or white)? That is, do both cards have white hair or black? Look at the second pair. Does the hair match or not?
3. Add up the number of pairs with matching hair. You may have one, two, or zero matching pairs. Write that number down.
4. Now do the same thing, but with the glasses this time. How many pairs match (glasses or no glasses)? Write that number next to the first one you've written.

5. Do the same thing again, this time with smiles or frowns. Write the number down. You should now have a three digit number such as "012."
6. Look up that number on the Talent List. You'll find a comment that applies to the card you laid to one side. That comment applies only to that one card, but for most cards there are several comments. Try the game again by reshuffling the cards or picking a new card to put to one side.

After the Game: Play several rounds. Ask students to tell their favorite answer from the Talent List.

TEACHING IDEAS

Materials Needed:

Object lesson: TV Guide.
Learning project: varies with the talent you choose for the students to experiment with.

Discussion Starters: Do you think God has given talents to everyone? Name some talents. Which one would you most like to have? What would you have to do to develop that talent? (For example, piano skills require much practice.) How could you use your favorite talent to honor God? (An artist could draw for the church newsletter.)

Object Lesson: Show a *TV Guide* or similar magazine to your learners. Explain, **This magazine is put together by a lot of talented people. And it's about television, which also involves a lot of talented people. I'm going to think of all the different jobs required to put this magazine and a TV show together. You help me out by saying any you think of and also by counting the jobs we come up with.** For the magazine, list writers, photographers, editors, proofreaders, designers, typesetters, artists, and anyone else you or your students can think of. A TV show requires writers, actors, producers, di-

rectors, musicians, and so on. Discuss the idea that the talents displayed in these jobs, as well as all others, are gifts from God that can and should be used to honor him.

Learning Project: Pick one of the things mentioned in the Talent List and do it. Number 202 would be especially fun. Create different musical notes by filling bottles with different amounts of water. Give each student a bottle to play. If you have many students, assemble them into "bands" to play six or eight bottles. Have them play "Mary Had a Little Lamb" or "Jesus Loves Me." Give tongue-in-cheek awards for the best and worst noise produced.

Conclusion Activity: Read the first part of 1 Peter 4:10: "Each one should use whatever gift he has received to serve others." Help your students plan a simple party that you can have next time. Each person contributes something to the party that represents the talent he or she has or would like to have. The musically inclined can bring music tapes, the cartoonists can put together a funny invitation or poster, some students can do a skit, and so on.

So Talented!

"His master replied, 'Well done, good and faithful servant! You have been faithful with a few things; I will put you in charge of many things. Come and share your master's happiness!'" (Matthew 25:21).

Talent List

The following list suggests ways to use the talents God has given different people.

000   Make a funny music video with classmates.
001   Draw cartoons for your church bulletin.
002   James 5:13 says, "Is anyone happy? Let him sing songs of praise."
010   Fill your brain with memorized Bible verses.
012   Use your brain to think up Bible games for friends.
020   Ephesians 5:19 says, "Sing and make music in your heart to the Lord."
021   Draw a Bible story cartoon for your classmates to read.
022   Write and perform a simple song for Jesus.
100   Get a video camera and make a Bible skit with pals.
102   Star in a Bible skit.
111   You're wrong! God has given you talents to use for him. Ask your parents or teacher to help you find them.
120   Put together a talent show with your classmates.
122   Give the class announcements with sound effects and silly motions.
200   Help your teacher pick good Christian music for class sing-alongs.
201   Make posters for your classroom.
202   Organize a bottle orchestra (people blow on partly full bottles).
210   Use your brains to think up a Bible skit.
212   Daniel 2:21 says that God gives wisdom to the wise.
220   Do the class announcements as a silly song.
221   Draw invitations to a fun church activity.
222   Help lead songs in your class.

Talent Cards

20. Christ's Death and Resurrection

Bible Passage: Matthew 27:27-28:15 and parallel
passages.
Lesson Theme: Some of the events surrounding
Christ's death and resurrection.

STORY

Story Starter: You can do the Object Lesson first, or simply start with the story.

Let's pretend that we've all been thrown into a military jail filled with soldiers doing time. These are Roman soldiers from long ago, for this small cell holds the officers and enlisted men who were assigned to guard Jesus just before and just after he was crucified on the cross. One frustrated officer stands and paces the tiny room.

1. "I tell you, it's unfair. The accusations against us are not fair! How can we help it if Jesus escaped from us?"

2. A tired soldier slumped against the wall speaks up. "Just where did our troubles begin, sir?"

1. "Well, the first time I saw Jesus, he had been arrested and charged with blasphemy by the Jewish high priest," says the officer.

3. "Blasphemy, sir? What's that?" asks another soldier.

1. "Jesus claimed to be the Son of God," explains the officer. "It's been said that he claimed that people could only go to heaven if they believed in him."

4. "I was there, too," says a soldier chained to the far wall. "When Jesus was arrested, I mean. He said that he was the king of the Jews. So we stripped him naked and covered him with a scarlet robe, like a king might wear. Someone brought a thin branch from a thorn bush—you know, the kind with the two-inch thorns? We made a crown out of it and jammed it down on his head. Then we made him hold a stick like a king's scepter. Everyone laughed and jeered. We bowed down and said, 'Hail, king of the Jews!' Then we all spit on him and hit him on the head again and again with the stick."

1. The officer speaks again. "The next time I saw Jesus, he was hanging on the cross, dying."

5. "That's right," says another. "I tried to give him wine to drink, mixed with gall—you know, that drug that women sometimes give to prisoners who are about to be crucified. It kills the pain. But Jesus wouldn't have it; I guess he wanted to be fully conscious until he died. I don't know why."

2. "What happened next?" the tired soldier asks.

6. "We cast lots for his clothes," says an old soldier. "He had good quality stuff. I won his coat."

Everyone falls silent, lost in thought, remembering the things that had been done to the one who claimed to be the Son of God.

(DEEP VOICE) 7. From the darkest corner of the dungeon, a centurion speaks in a deep, pain-filled voice. "I remember what happened that day. It is forever burned into my memory."

7. After a long pause, the centurion continues. "As we crucified him, as we nailed him to the cross, he looked at us and said, 'Father, forgive them, for they do not know what they are doing.' Then he spoke to another man who was being crucified. He promised that they would be together in paradise that very day. I'll never forget, never."

The soldiers are all looking at their feet.

7. The centurion speaks again. "The sun stopped shining. It was the middle of the day and it grew pitch dark. Jesus cried out in a loud voice, then he died. There was an earthquake. We were terrified. I said it then, and I say it now: He was the Son of God!"

The centurion sobs in the gloom, shaking with grief.

1. "Son of God, Centurion? Nonsense!" scoffs the officer pacing the cell. "If he were really God's son, would he have died such a miserable death? I will not believe in one who lays dead in the grave."

7. "Then perhaps," says the centurion, "you will believe in one who has risen from that grave. The tomb is empty. That's why we are here now."

1. "We are here now," shouts the officer, "because Jesus' body was stolen from that tomb!"

But no one listens to the officer. They all know the truth. Jesus' body had been laid in a cave carved into the solid rock. A huge stone had been rolled across the entrance. The stone had been sealed with an official emblem, and they had been posted to guard the tomb against any possible vandalism. No one had come.

No one had come, that is, until an angel from God appeared with an earthquake and rolled open the stone. The guards were so afraid they shook and became like dead men. When they came to, there was no angel. And there was no body of Christ.

The soldiers reported what had happened. The chief priests, the ones who had ordered Jesus' arrest, paid the soldiers a large sum of money to lie about what they had seen. The soldiers agreed to report that Jesus' disciples had stolen the body by night, as the soldiers slept.

We don't know if the soldiers that had been at Jesus' tomb really were sent to prison for "losing" Jesus' body. Normally, a soldier who let a prisoner escape would have been thrown in jail or executed. But we do know this—after that day, hundreds of people saw Jesus alive. They spoke with him, ate with him, and watched as he, some weeks later, rose up into the clouds and out of their sight. Many of these same witnesses died for their faith. What they saw really happened. If it hadn't, these people would not have allowed themselves to be tortured and killed for the man who claimed to be the Son of God.

GAME INSTRUCTIONS

Materials Needed: One photocopy of the game per player, pencils.

Approximate Playing Time: 10-15 minutes.

Special Instructions: Hand out a photocopy of the game to each player. Read aloud the game's entire Bible passage as students follow along. Make sure they understand that the answers to the crossword clues are found in the passage. See the crossword solution at the end of the book.

TEACHING IDEAS

Materials Needed:

Object lesson: empty, gift-wrapped box; an unwrapped prize.

Learning project: poster boards, pens, cellophane tape, index cards labeled with one word per card.

Discussion Starters:
(If your students do the Learning Project, ask these questions afterward.) What did Jesus do that demonstrates his love for us? What claim did Jesus make that so infuriated the Jewish leaders? In what ways does Jesus coming to life from the grave prove that the Jewish leaders were wrong about him?

Object Lesson:
Allow a volunteer to unwrap a beautiful gift box—to find it empty. Tell your students, *One of the greatest gifts ever given was the empty tomb of Jesus Christ. This box is empty just as his grave is empty. Why is that such a great gift? Because it means that his death on the cross to forgive our sins was honored by God. Because Jesus died and rose from the dead, we have a living Savior in heaven. A great gift indeed.*

To soften the blow to the volunteer's ego, give him or her a soda or other prize in place of the empty box.

Learning Project:
Your learners are going to play an action game that will result in two posters to display in your classroom. Each poster features one of the verses below.

"Greater love has no one than this, that he lay down his life for his friends" (John 15:13).

"But God demonstrates his own love for us in this: While we were still sinners, Christ died for us" (Romans 5:8).

At the top of a sheet of poster paper or board, label the first part of John 15:13, like this: *John 15:13—Greater love has no one than this.* . . . On the second poster write, *Romans 5:8—But God demonstrates his own love for us in this:*

Gather the students together into two teams, lined up single file. Give each team a tape dispenser and a set of nine index cards on which you've written the missing words, one word per card. On one team's cards are written the words from John 15:13, on the other team's cards the words from Romans 5:8. Each player should receive one card. Double up cards if you have less than nine players per team. Extra students can watch and help solve the puzzle.

Explain, *The object of our game is to be the first team to correctly complete the Bible verse. Team #1 does John 15:13; team #2 does Romans 5:8. When I give the signal to go, I want the first person in line on each team to take his or her card, run to the assigned poster, and tape the card to the poster. Each player runs back and tags the next person who then tapes his or her word to the poster. At first, it will be impossible to know the correct order the cards should be in. But as more and more cards are taped up, soon you can begin to rearrange them to make sense. The first team to do so wins.*

Feel free to drop big hints as teams struggle to guess the order of the words. It's likely that teams will not be completely accurate. Give the victory to whichever team seems to understand the meaning of the verse. Talk through Discussion Starters.

Christ's Crossword

They came to a place called Golgotha (which means The Place of the Skull). When they had crucified him, they divided up his clothes by casting lots.
And when Jesus had cried out again in a loud voice, he gave up his spirit. At that moment the curtain of the temple was torn in two from top to bottom. The earth shook and the rocks split. The tombs broke open and the bodies of many holy people who had died were raised to life.
When the centurion and those with him who were guarding Jesus saw the earthquake and all that had happened, they were terrified, and exclaimed, "Surely he was the Son of God!"
After the Sabbath, at dawn on the first day of the week, Mary Magdalene and the other Mary went to look at the tomb. There was a violent earthquake, for an angel of the Lord came down from heaven and, going to the tomb, rolled back the stone and sat on it.
The angel said to the women, "Do not be afraid, for I know that you are looking for Jesus, who was crucified. He is not here; he has risen, just as he said. Come and see the place where he lay" (Matthew 27:33, 35, 50-52, 54; 28:1, 2, 5, 6).

This crossword puzzle features many of the words about Jesus' death and resurrection found in the Bible passage above. The answers to the clues are in the passage.

ACROSS

4. The place where they crucified Jesus.
7. He told the women that Jesus was alive.
8. This was rolled back by the angel.
9. The soldiers did this to Jesus' clothes.
11. Golgotha means this.
14. The soldiers did this to Jesus.
15. This happened to the tombs of many holy men.
16. Jesus gave this up.

DOWN

1. The angel did this to the stone.
2. The soldiers cast these for Jesus' clothes.
3. The rocks split and the earth did this.
5. Mary's last name.
6. He guarded Jesus and said, "Surely he was the Son of God!"
10. Jesus cried out with this.
12. The angel told the women not to be this.
13. When the centurion and others saw the earthquake, they felt this.

Solution Sheet

Hark, an Ark!

There may be many pathways to the Ark.

Snakebit!

The A-Mazed Paralytic!

DRAW YOUR LINE THROUGH ALL OF THE OBSTACLES TO WIN!

Jesus Versus the Devil

G + pool + D - gold + C + water - cat = POWER
P + foot - pot + cork - fork - C + F = OF
bag + T - bat + toad + pole - tadpole + D = GOD

The Son of God

WORD, ROCK, TRUTH, WAY, MEDIATOR, SHEPHERD, PROPHET, LORD, LAMB, MESSIAH, COUNSELOR, DOOR, KING, LIFE, SAVIOR, GOD, LIGHT

Distractions, Distractions

Christ's Crossword